THE MEANING
OF THE CROSS

THE MEANING OF THE CROSS : A STUDY OF THE ATONEMENT

BY

EDWARD GRUBB, M.A.

Author of "The Religion of Experience," "Christ in
Christian Thought," "The Word made Flesh,"
"Authority and the Light Within," etc.

LONDON : GEORGE ALLEN & UNWIN LTD.
RUSKIN HOUSE, 40 MUSEUM STREET, W.C. 1

First published in 1922

PREFACE

THIS little book contains the substance of a course of lectures delivered at the Woodbrooke Settlement, near Birmingham, to a class of students from the sister institutions, Carey Hall, Kingsmead, West Hill and Woodbrooke, in the early part of 1921. Portions of some of the chapters have appeared in *The Friend*, to the Editor of which paper the author's thanks are due for permission to reprint them here.

While his treatment of the subject is the outcome of thought and study extending over many years, there is little or nothing for which the author can claim originality, and it would be useless therefore to attempt the acknowledgment of obligations. A word may, however, be added to indicate his view of the Bible and its authority. This he has recently endeavoured to set forth in a simple way in a small book, *The Bible, its Nature and Inspiration*, the following extracts from which will perhaps sufficiently suggest his point of view:

" The inspiration of the Bible is something

that we have to learn to recognise for ourselves.
It has real meaning for us as we come to per-
ceive and feel it—just as the beauty of a great
picture, or the power of a great poem, must be
felt and perceived by ourselves if for us it is to
be a reality.

" But the Bible contains a great deal of matter
which does not carry its own evidence of inspiration, and yet there is a real sense in which we
can, and must, speak of the inspiration of the
Bible as a whole. What we have to lay hold
of is a thread that runs all through it, and connects together its least impressive parts with
those that move and inspire us. That thread is
to be found in the conviction, with which the
open-minded study of the Bible leaves us, that
it is the record of *a great Divine process,* which
reached its culmination in the person and work
of Jesus Christ. The Bible is man's record of
a Divine revelation, it is not the revelation
itself. We cannot find in it a final and infallible
standard of truth or duty. The Bible is indeed
full of God, and in a real sense it all points to
Christ, who is the expression of God in terms of
humanity ; but being man's record, it is full of
imperfection. We cannot use it *mechanically,*
when we seek in it guidance on our problems,
as though all parts of it were on one level of
Divine infallibility. To try to do so is to shut

our eyes to the very gradual process by which men's thoughts of God were cleared and deepened, to the imperfection of men's apprehension of what God was making known to them, and to the necessary limitations of human language when they strove to express the best that they had apprehended.

" The truth is that the Bible contains no single and uniform answer to any of the great questions that we may ask. We are not setting aside its authority when we say that it can only be rightly used, for establishing the doctrines of Christianity, and for meeting the attacks of unbelievers or the perplexities of those in doubt, by those who have made some careful study of what it really is, and what are the different strains of teaching which it contains. Such a treatment does not undermine or set aside the authority of Scripture, but shows us how it can be livingly appealed to. We trace the growing and deepening convictions of inspired seers and teachers, and read them in the light of the revelation brought by Jesus Christ himself, which answers to the deepest demands of our own reason and conscience."

EDWARD GRUBB.

LETCHWORTH,
December 1921.

CONTENTS

CHAPTER III

CHAPTER IV

CHAPTER V

CHAPTER VIII

The Meaning of the Cross

CHAPTER I

INTRODUCTORY

The Meaning of Atonement

The word "Atonement" is not found in the English New Testament, except in the Authorised Version of Romans v. 11, where the Revisers have substituted the word "reconciliation." This is obviously an improvement, because the noun (*katallagē*) corresponds to the verb "to reconcile" (*katallassein*), which has been twice used in the preceding verse:

> "For if, while we were enemies, we were reconciled to God through the death of His Son, much more, being reconciled, shall we be saved by his life; and not only so, but we also rejoice in God through our Lord Jesus Christ, through whom we have now received the reconciliation."

That was the meaning of Atonement in Elizabethan days: it meant bringing two estranged persons together, and making them "at one." Shakspeare always uses it in this sense, for example in *Richard III*, Act I, Scene 3:

> "He desires to make atonement
> Between the Duke of Gloucester and your brothers."

And *Richard II*, Act I, Scene 1 :

> " Since we cannot atone you."

The idea of " atoning " for a crime by making reparation, or suffering a punishment for it, is a later one.

In the Old Testament the phrase " to make atonement " is of frequent occurrence. In the next chapter we shall be considering whether and how far it bears the later meaning ; meanwhile I wish in this chapter to say a few words about what we call " the Atonement." I propose to use the word in its general Christian sense, namely *the relation of the suffering and death of Jesus Christ to human salvation*, and, in particular, to the forgiveness of sins by God. The definition takes for granted, in accordance with the Christian tradition, that there is such a relation ; but it does not assume at the outset that any particular doctrine about the nature of the relation is the only one that can be rightly held. Many of us were taught in early life that God forgives our sins because Jesus Christ bore in our stead the punishment which they deserved —subject, of course, to our acceptance of that substitutionary sacrifice. But this is only one of the ways in which, during the centuries, Christians have thought of the relation of Christ's death to human salvation. We want a definition of Atonement that shall be broad enough to cover these other ways ; and I hope the one I have chosen will leave the road open for studying some of them.

THE DOCTRINE OF SUBSTITUTION

The particular theory known as " the Doctrine of Substitution " has, in the main, held the field in Christian thought and experience since the Reformation—that is to say, among Protestants. In the Roman Church no single way of defining the Atonement has had such a dominant place. But the doctrine of Substitution has become, for many earnest minds, simply incredible ; and there is a widespread desire for some explanation that can be believed. For this change in our outlook there are various reasons.

(1) In the first place, the sense of personal *sin* is less acute in most of us than it was in our forefathers, and consequently many of us do not feel the need of forgiveness in the way they did. We see plenty of wrong and evil in the world of human life, and in the institutions of human society, but we have more difficulty in seeing just what is wrong with ourselves.

(2) Some well-meaning people tell us this does not matter. Sin, they say, is not a reality, but

is entirely due to wrong thoughts. If we get rid of illusions, and think rightly (they seem to assume that this is quite an easy thing to do), all will be well. It is obvious that this teaching hardly finds a place for Atonement in any sense.

(3) But many people who do feel sin acutely, and with it the need of Divine forgiveness, cannot think it right or just that the innocent should be punished instead of the guilty : their deepest moral instincts revolt ; and they cannot reconcile the thought of a God who acts in this way with the picture of the Father of whom Jesus taught, and in communion with whom he lived.

(4) Besides, our thought of Salvation has deepened. We feel that the main thing is not to escape from punishment, even in the next world, but *to escape from sin* and to be able to live rightly in this world. When the Atonement is presented as a means of escaping punishment, the need for right living seems to take a secondary place, whereas we feel it ought to have the first place. But it is not clear to us how an event that happened long ago can help us in our moral struggle to-day. Perhaps it can ; but the connection is not obvious. It cannot be explained on a tract, as the old doctrine could.

(5) Behind all this there is an enlarged thought of God. We are not satisfied to think of Him as a magnified Judge, dealing out penalties at His own will. We have begun to understand, better than our forefathers, that He works through "natural law," and that the punishments of sin are, as St. Paul taught, its natural consequences—"whatsoever a man soweth, that shall he also reap." It is not easy to see how such natural consequences of wrongdoing *could* be transferred to another person, even were it right that they should be.

(6) To some, perhaps, the most fundamental difficulty arises from the discovery of Evolution. We have most of us come to believe in the gradual upward progress of mankind from a savage ancestry, and, behind that, from lower forms of animal life. Not only do our minds refuse belief in the historic reality of the "Fall" recorded in Genesis; the idea of Sin itself may seem to be inconsistent with that of Evolution. The whole world of ideas with which Atonement is connected begins to some people to appear as one of myth and not of reality.

THE NEED OF A BETTER DOCTRINE

The result of all this is that "the Gospel," as it has often been preached, does not fit our experience nor meet our spiritual needs. Perhaps

we imagine it is taught in the Bible, but we
cannot really believe it, and so the Bible loses
its hold on us. Or, if we still cling to the belief
that it must be true in *some* sense, we cannot
make clear to ourselves in *what* sense, and so
we let it alone. We are not satisfied to use
conventional phrases unless they really mean
something to us : like David when offered Saul's
armour we say, " I cannot go with these, for I
have not proved them " (1 Sam. xvii. 39). And
so, as no believable doctrine of Atonement is
presented to us, and we cannot discover one
for ourselves, we simply cease to think about it.

But if, as I for one profoundly believe, the
Cross of Christ is the very centre of the Christian
life, this leaving out of the Atonement means,
inevitably, spiritual impoverishment. And there
is reason to believe that many individual lives,
and many Churches also, are seriously im-
poverished to-day just on this account. There
are devout Christian ministers who are unable
to deal with the redemptive power of the suffering and death of Christ, even though they
vaguely feel that it is the centre of the Gospel—
because they have found no way of stating the
matter which satisfies them, or which they can
ask other people to believe.[1]

[1] See David Smith, *The Atonement in the Light of History
and the Modern Spirit*, Preface ; and Douglas White, *Forgiveness and Suffering*, pp. 2–5.

My own assurance is that, through the labours
of many earnest and spiritually-minded Christian
thinkers, we are on the way to a solution of
this problem : to a doctrine which, though doubtless not complete or final, is yet deep enough,
simple enough and rich enough to meet the
intellectual and spiritual needs of men to-day,
and which at the same time is in fundamental
agreement with the real teaching of the Bible—
that is to say, with the deepest thoughts reached
by its writers under the progressive illumination
of God's Spirit, and, most of all, with the
character of the Father revealed in Jesus Christ.
But, before attempting to study the teaching
of the Bible about Atonement, or the explanations given by Christians at different periods,
it will be well to try to clear out of the way one
or two difficulties which, for some thoughtful
people, stand in the way of any doctrine on
this subject. Belief in Atonement in any sense
seems to require acceptance first of the reality
of Sin, and secondly of the idea of Personality
in God ; but these foundations some find it
hard to lay.

PRESUPPOSITIONS : (*a*) THE REALITY OF SIN

It is obvious that, unless Sin is a real evil,
there is no place for Redemption, and the basis
is gone for any doctrine of Atonement what-

ever. We must face the question whether acceptance of belief in Evolution is inconsistent with belief in the reality of Sin. I do not think it is. Even if, as we must, we take the Eden story as poetry and not history, it still gives us in pictorial form a true account of what has really happened in the experience of the human race. The development of persons from the world of animal life has meant that intelligence and free choice have, in the main, replaced blind instinct as the source and condition of man's activity. His intelligence has been *misused*, as instinct is not misused. An animal's instinctive impulses drive it along the path it has to take, and it has no power to resist them. It does, speaking broadly, and allowing for possible exceptions as instinct approaches intelligence, fulfil the law of its being, and so its life is a harmony. I believe it is true to say that no animal, in a state of nature, ever eats so much as to suffer from indigestion. An ant or a bee cannot do other than work for the community in which it lives. But, when self-consciousness develops, it becomes possible to make self and its satisfaction the aim to which action is directed, even if this (temporary) satisfaction is secured by violating the true order of our life, and sacrificing the real interests of the community. We can and do put what we take to be our own interests above those of the whole of which we form a part, and this is Sin.

Sin is not, therefore, as is sometimes said, "the remains of our animal nature," for animals (again speaking broadly) do not sin. The cuckoo, indeed, looks like a selfish unsociable creature— especially when it lays its egg in another bird's nest, and the young cuckoo, when hatched, heaves out of the nest the rightful occupants. This tendency to take the easy way of living at the expense of others is known as *Parasitism*, and is indeed deeply embedded in the animal and vegetable worlds. It does appear to be akin to that tendency which, in intelligent beings, we call Sin ; but it is not Sin, because it is not the outcome of free choice. We cannot blame the individual cuckoo for taking the easy way, any more than we can praise the salmon which is driven along the hard way of swimming against the current, and leaping waterfalls, that it may find the spawning-ground to perpetuate its race. Neither creature can do other than it does. Each fulfils the law of its being, even though that law, in the case of the cuckoo, does not seem to be altogether a good one.

Sin does not appear until, in the course of Evolution, we reach the stage of intelligence and self-conscious personality. It marks a fall below the animal level, even though the intel-

ligence which makes sin possible means a rise;
for the perversion of the best is ever the worst.
Every true observer of human life has noted
how sadly it differs from the happy instinctive
life of the animals, how the harmony has been
turned into discord because the performers have
gone their own way instead of following the
mind of the Composer.

" O dreary life, we cry, O dreary life !
    And still the generations of the birds
    Sing through our sighing, still the flocks and herds
    Serenely dwell, while we are keeping strife
    With God's true purpose in us, like a knife
    Against which we may struggle."

' I think I could turn and live with the animals, they
        are so placid and self-contained ;
They do not lie awake in the dark and weep for their sins ;
Not one is dissatisfied, not one is demented with the mania
        of owning things,
Not one is respectable or unhappy over the whole earth."

If any of us, before the Great War, doubted
the reality of Sin, we can surely doubt it
no longer.   The world is well-nigh in ruins ;
humanity has clearly missed its way.   The present
Bishop of Manchester wrote some wise words,
even before the war, about " the horror of our
present European civilisation," and the fact
that " the origin of the whole horror is simply

that people, speaking generally, are as good as we are and not better." [1]

And we all, if we are honest, know this to be true by looking steadily within our own hearts. We know well that we have often missed our way, that we have freely chosen the easier path when the law of our being bade us take the harder. It is our *will* that is wrong ; it is not so much " I would do right but I can't," as " I could do right but I won't "—I will not, that is, with my whole self, though partly I desire it. " Give me chastity," prayed St. Augustine, " but not yet." And, as sin is a disease of the will, it admits of no cure by any self-acting " natural " process. It is not natural, but *un-natural*, and the remedy must be more than natural. Sin cannot be cured by force or compulsion. That may in measure prevent the wrong act being done, but it cannot remove the

---

[1] " If you take some millions of people just like ourselves, generous up to a point, but still predominantly selfish, with varying abilities, and leave them to live together for several generations, the result will be something like the horror of our present European civilisation. The sin that has made it is just our sin. That is what our sort of character works out at if you leave it alone. There is no need for the modern man to feel self-complacent about his character or to ' cease to worry about his sins.' If he will go into the poorer parts of any big town or into some of the more starved villages of the country, and will reflect that what he sees arises because the majority of people are just like himself, he will find he has plenty of room for real penitence, and plenty of need for new power."—W. Temple, *The Kingdom of God*, pp. 75, 76.

will to do it. Only if the good is freely chosen is sin really overcome. This means that *a new motive* is required, which can change and move and inspire the will to choose the good. And it is here that Christ and his Cross have proved dynamic for the world's redemption.

(b) THE PERSONALITY OF GOD

Such considerations may suffice to show the reality of Sin and the need of Redemption; but Atonement implies something more. It involves, as we have seen, reconciliation, which can only mean the restoration of right relations between persons. Indeed, Sin itself only acquires its real ugliness when it is seen to be more than a disease; when it is looked on as unfilial conduct, an outrage on love, something (as has been said) as loathsome as hitting one's mother in the face. It is when we see it in the light of personal relations, as in the case of the Prodigal Son, that we understand what it really means. In the impersonal religions, like Buddhism, there is no forgiveness and no Atonement. The real problem of Atonement is the restoration of right personal relations between God and man. But this involves the thought of personality in God, which some of us may find it hard to hold. If so, we must remember that our finite human personality is not the measure of the Divine;

perhaps we finite beings, if we are followers of God and goodness, are rather on the road to achieving true personality than already persons in the full sense. God *is* that which we are to *become*. He is described, in the most inspired words about Him that we have, as *Love*; but Love, apart from a loving person, is only an abstraction, and God is certainly not that. Tolstoy says, " Where love is, God is "; and this is true in the sense that all real love is an expression of His nature. It is not true if we take it to mean that God is only an abstraction —the name for a certain quality of human beings. If the word " God " is to have meaning, it must stand for a concrete reality—indeed for the reality which alone enables us to call anything real.

We have not to belittle our idea of God in order to think of Him as personal. The remedy for our difficulty is not to narrow our thought of Him, but to enlarge our idea of what Personality means. And the modern study of Psychology—that is, of persons—enables us, indeed compels us, to do this. For it proves that even our human personality is a great deal larger than we had supposed : that behind and beneath our fully conscious life there lies an immeasurable region of ourselves of which we are normally not conscious. This is known as the subconscious or subliminal part of our mysterious personality ; and it is in this region, as all the recent investigation of Telepathy assures us, that we come into the most intimate relations with other personalities.

A Person is simply a *Self* that can say " I " and " me " : a being that can feel and think and will ; the word does not necessarily imply the limitation of a physical organism, or the separation from other conscious beings which our normal experience suggests to us. The more deeply we study the subject, the more we shall be convinced that there is something of the Infinite in us all ; and that to speak of an Infinite Person is by no means the contradiction that at first it seems to be. It will, indeed, be probably found that a true philosophy necessarily leads us up to the thought of a Universal Consciousness, of which our finite minds are but a partial and as yet inadequate expression : that, as was said above, we are (in so far as we have the life of God in us) on the way to achieving personality as it is in Him.

But we have not to wait for this achievement, or for a clear apprehension of what Personality in God means, before we can lay hold of the Cross of Christ. It is *he* who has revealed to us, like no other, the personality and character of God ; and the only way to make that revelation our own is to strive to live as if it were true, and to verify it in our lives by proving that our experience is what it would be if the revelation were true. "No one," says Mr. Clutton-Brock, "has a right to more faith than he has earned; and the only way to earn faith is to act upon it before it comes." [1]

We need, not, therefore, abandon the search for a true doctrine of the Cross on the ground that it involves an idea of God which we have not yet made our own. The more Christ and his Cross become a living part of our own experience, the nearer shall we be able to rise to his thought of God, of the reality of Sin, and of the meaning of Atonement.

[1] *More Thoughts on the War*, p. 82.

CHAPTER II

ATONEMENT IN THE OLD TESTAMENT

WHY THE OLD TESTAMENT MUST BE CONSIDERED

IT has been held that, while the Substitutionary idea of Atonement is clearly taught by St. Paul and other New Testament writers, this is because they had not thrown off the Jewish notions in which they had been trained. The assumption is that these ideas were taught in the Old Testament, but were discarded by Jesus Christ, though not by his followers. Now it is certain that these followers, and their Master before them, regarded the Scriptures of their people with the greatest reverence, as containing " the oracles of God " (Rom. iii. 2) ; and indeed Christianity can never be properly understood apart from its sources in Hebrew and Jewish religion. Hence the importance of devoting some study to Old Testament ideas of Atonement.

At the same time, we must beware of supposing that the Gospel can be explained by the Law, or even by the Prophets. There was a progress in revelation, a development of ideas ; and we must try to judge the lower ideas in the

light of the higher, and not *vice versa*. Jesus
is reported to have said that he came " to fulfil
the law and the prophets " (Matt. v. 17) ; by
which he doubtless meant that his Gospel was
the legitimate development of the Law, as the
flower is of the bud. We must not try to explain
the New Testament by Leviticus, or even by
the fifty-third chapter of Isaiah, as if these Old
Testament law-books and prophecies were intended to clear up points that the New Testament leaves obscure. We do not understand
the meaning of the Old Testament better than
that of the New ; on the contrary, it is a matter
of no small difficulty to recover with certainty
the thoughts of the ancient Hebrew and Jewish
writers, and to interpret correctly what they
meant by the practices of their religion and the
glowing words of their prophecies.

The Practice of Sacrifice

Two opposing facts strike us in studying the
Old Testament : first, that Hebrew religion (including that of the Jews after the Exile) expressed itself very largely in the practice of
Sacrifice ; and second, that the greater prophets
and psalmists very frequently denounced the
abuses of the sacrificial system. So strong is
their denunciation that it is still debated by
students whether it was only the abuses they

objected to, or whether they did not regard the whole sacrificial system as a mistake.[1] What they urge is that the only sacrifice really pleasing to Jehovah is the surrender of the life to the doing of His will.[2]

Modern study of the Old Testament has made it impossible to think of the elaborate system of sacrifice, enjoined in such law-books as Leviticus, as having been directly ordained by God. It is found that sacrifice in general was common to the Hebrews and to other Semitic tribes, and that even some of the particular practices of the Hebrews had their analogues in other religions. Further, sacrifice in some form is found in primitive religion generally. The Hebrew historians themselves did not think of sacrifice as having been *first* instituted under Moses. They represent it as quite primitive, as having been practised by Cain and Abel (Gen. iv. 2 ff.), by Noah (Gen. viii. 20), and so on. What apparently happened was that religious leaders and legislators, like Moses and Ezra, men who felt themselves

[1] Note, among many passages, Amos v. 21–24, Hos. vi. 6, Isa. i. 11–17, and especially Jer. vii. 22, 23 : " For I spake not unto your fathers, nor commanded them in the day that I brought them out of the land of Egypt, concerning burnt offerings or sacrifices ; but this thing I commanded them, saying, Hearken unto My voice, and I will be your God, and ye shall be My people." In the light of modern study of the practice of sacrifice, it seems very probable that Jeremiah meant exactly what he said.

[2] Ps. xl. 6–8 ; l. 13, 14 ; li. 16, 17, etc.

to be acting under Divine control and direction, took up and adapted certain existing practices, purifying them of corrupt and demoralising elements, and giving them a deeper and more ethical meaning and purpose.

The great elaboration of sacrifice which we find in Leviticus and Numbers is now believed to have been a late and not an early development ; probably in the main it is post-exilic.[1] The kernel of the Mosaic legislation, whether actually as old as the time of Moses or not, is to be found in Exodus xx.–xxiii. A point of much importance is that in this legislation sacrifice might be offered *anywhere* where there was a "holy place" (Ex. xx. 24)—that is, in almost any village. Not till after Josiah's reformation (about 621 B.C.) was it confined to the Temple at Jerusalem. This reformation was based on the "book of the law" found in the Temple, which is believed to have been part or the whole of the Book of Deuteronomy. In this book it is clearly laid down that sacrifice is *not* to be

---

[1] The first captivity of the Jews was in 598 B.C., the second in 586. On each occasion Nebuchadnezzar took some thousands of them to Babylon. On the second, Jerusalem and the Temple were destroyed. The return began under Cyrus after 538. Many of the people of the Northern Kingdom had been carried away by the Assyrians as early as 722 B.C. These never returned. Apparently they abandoned their distinctive religion and were absorbed into other nations. The "lost ten tribes" are in all probability lost for ever.

offered " in every place that thou seest, but in the place which the Lord shall choose in one of thy tribes " (Deut. xii. 13, 14). The development of the priestly and sacrificial system is believed to have been largely due to Ezra the priest, who came to Jerusalem from Babylon in 458 B.C., and read before the people the " book of the law " about the year 444. It may have been thought out in part by Ezekiel and other priests during the Exile.

The Meaning of Sacrifice

Sacrifice in ancient times was not always or necessarily connected with the sense of sin. Its essential idea seems to have been an offering or present to the God, to keep in touch with Him and retain His favour. Especially it was *a common meal*, shared by the God and His worshippers, which created or renewed the bond between them. The sharing of food established a bond of fellowship ; even to this day " table communion " is regarded by Arabs as a solemn and sacred thing, and they will not injure a man with whom they have recently eaten. Hence sacrifice was usually, and on the whole, a *joyous* thing. But at times, especially under calamity, when it was feared the God might be hostile, special and costly offerings were made to procure His favour, even in the shape of human sacrifices. Recent discoveries have proved that these were common among the Canaanites.

The early Hebrew sacrifices were on the whole similar to those used by other Semitic tribes. They differed chiefly in the conception of the *character* of the God who was worshipped. From very early times the Hebrews were taught by their leaders, doubtless with Divine help and inspiration, a higher ethical conception of Jehovah than those which prevailed in regard to other Gods. We note in particular, in Gen. xxii., the revelation to Abraham that human sacrifice was not acceptable to Jehovah. In the law-books the note of a joyous eating with Jehovah is frequently struck, especially in Deuteronomy, as in xii. 7 : " there ye shall eat before Jehovah your God, and ye shall rejoice in all that ye put your hand unto, ye and your households." Though the idea of Jehovah actually sharing in the meal does not appear here, in other passages (chiefly in Leviticus) sacrifice is several times called His " food " or " bread " ; as in Lev. iii. 11, " it is the food of the offering made by fire unto Jehovah," and xxi. 6, " for the offerings of Jehovah made by fire, the bread of their God, do they offer." The " shewbread," or " bread of the presence," in 1 Sam. xxi. 1–6, etc., was doubtless originally intended as a meal for Jehovah.

The practice here alluded to, of burning the sacrifice, is, I believe, not found except among the Hebrews. The Canaanites were accustomed to pour out the blood of the victim upon the altar, but not to burn its flesh.[1] The burning of part of the victim was probably due to the idea that as it disappeared in smoke and steam the unseen Deity could more easily have His share. (Note the expression in Gen. viii. 21, etc., " and Jehovah smelled the sweet savour.")

The Hebrew nation was very early taught to regard itself as in " a covenant relation " with Jehovah. We have, for example, the solemn agreement made with Abraham, described in Gen. xv., when as " the sun went down, and it was dark, behold a smoking furnace and a flaming torch," representing the presence of Jehovah, " passed between the pieces " of the victims which Abraham had prepared. The covenant is solemnly renewed by Moses and the " elders," on behalf of the people, with sprinkling of the blood of the victims, in Ex. xxiv. 1–11, where the passage ends, " and they beheld God, and did eat and drink." The sacrificial meal thus renewed from time to time the bond that united

---

[1] See Article " Canaanites " in *Encyclopædia of Religion and Ethics*, vol. iii., p. 176–188. It is stated (p. 187) that " parts of the animal were given to the God by throwing them into a pit, *or by burning.*" No evidence, however, of the latter practice is given, while there are many evidences of receptacles for the blood of the victims.

Jehovah with His people : they could rejoice in His favour and His help, and renewed their promise to serve Him faithfully in obedience to His moral requirements.

SACRIFICE AS EXPIATION FOR SIN

So far, there is but little to connect the practice of sacrifice with the sense of sin or with atonement. Even in early days, however, this element was not absent. Note, for example, 1 Sam. iii. 14, " Therefore have I sworn that the iniquity of Eli's house shall not be purged with sacrifice nor offering for ever." Also 2 Sam. xxiv. 25, " And David built there an altar unto Jehovah, and offered burnt offerings and peace offerings. So Jehovah was intreated for the land, and the plague was stayed." As trouble and disaster came more heavily on the nation, and as a profounder consciousness of the Divine holiness was awakened by the teachings of the prophets, the sense of sin deepened among the people, and the need of expiation took a stronger hold of their minds. This was especially so after the crowning calamity of the Exile, which, as they were assured by prophets like Jeremiah and Ezekiel, had come upon them as a chastisement for their sins. Hence it was that there arose that elaborate system of expiatory sacrifice to which we have already alluded. Into

its complexities we cannot enter here. They
are probably due in part to the fact that the
system was worked out in detail by a succession
of priestly leaders, who not only modified existing arrangements, but added fresh features from
time to time. The law-books, as we have them,
are in all probability the result of putting together
various strata of priestly legislation.

All we can do is to try to catch the leading
and essential ideas. The expression " to make
atonement " is very frequent in our English
version, and is a translation of the Hebrew word
kipper. The exact meaning of this word is still
doubtful. Its Arabic equivalent, I am told,
means " to cover " ; the Syriac " to wipe away " ;
and the Assyrian " to purge by ritual." Whichever meaning is nearest to the Hebrew, it is
clear that the word refers to the removal of sin
out of the sight of Jehovah : that is to say,
*it is not used in the heathen sense of propitiating
Him or trying to gain His favour.* When the
expression " to make atonement " is used, it is
not in the sense of appeasing God.[1]

Sacrifice, then, was not thought of by the
Hebrew teachers and writers (whatever the

[1] The Septuagint version (the translation of the Hebrew
Bible into Greek) is very careful to observe this rule. The
only word the translators could find to render *kipper* was
exilaskesthai, which in pagan Greek would mean propitiating
a divinity ; but they carefully avoided putting after it the
word *Theon* (God).

popular conceptions about it may have been)
as intended to propitiate God. This is the vital
distinction between the Hebrew and the pagan
ideas. What it was believed to do was to remove
sin " before God "—that is, to put it out of His
sight. This is specially clear in the central
passage, Lev. xvi. 30, concerning the great Day
of Atonement :

"For on this day shall atonement be made for you
to cleanse you ; from all your sins shall ye be clean before
Jehovah."

The thought is that the sacrifice cleanses the
people : it was directed in the first instance
not to God, but to the people's sin. Yet there
was always the further reference to God which
is conveyed in the words "before Jehovah."
It was not the bare removal of sin without regard
to Him ; it was removing it out of His sight,
and so making possible the approach to Him
which sin blocked. Sacrifice was the principal
means by which the people were assured of His
forgiveness and of communion with Him.

Yet the distinction, vitally important as it
is, between the two ideas of propitiating God
and removing sin from His sight, was probably
too subtle for many simple minds to grasp ;
and it would seem that the pagan idea tended
continually to recur. Hence, perhaps, in part,
the vehemence of the prophetic denunciations

of the abuse of sacrifice.   And sometimes, though
very rarely, the writers themselves speak of
sacrifice as intended to avert Jehovah's wrath :
as in Ex. xxx. 12, " When thou takest the sum
of the children of Israel, then shall they give
every man a ransom for his soul unto the Lord,
that there be no plague among them when thou
numberest them." (Compare Num. viii. 19.)   In
these few cases the writers or legislators themselves would seem to have forgotten, or ignored,
the distinction which is generally kept so clear.

The Shedding of Blood

The writer of the Epistle to the Hebrews says
(ix. 22) : " According to the law, I may almost
say, all things are cleansed with blood, and
apart from shedding of blood there is no remission." While special emphasis was laid on blood-
shedding, this was not regarded as always necessary : a poor person who could not afford an
animal might bring meal as a sin offering
(Lev. v. 11). Usually the blood of the victim
brought as a sin offering was sprinkled on the
altar " before Jehovah," and sometimes on the
worshippers ; and the rest of it was poured out
at the base of the altar. A similar use of blood
is found, as was said above, in heathen sacrifices,
and it was regarded as most potent when it was
that of the worshippers themselves. This is why

the prophets of Baal in the Elijah story "cut themselves after their manner with knives and lances, till the blood gushed out upon them" (1 Kings xviii. 28). They no doubt attributed to the blood some magic efficacy; and similar ideas probably had a place in popular Hebrew thought. But the writers of the Old Testament had to a large extent risen above purely magical conceptions. Yet they never *explain* what the efficacy of the blood was thought to be—perhaps it never occurred to them that anyone would think of asking for an explanation. The nearest approach to one is in Lev. xvii. 11, but here it is only indirect, since what the writer gives us is the reason why blood must not be *eaten*:

"For the life (or soul) of the flesh is in the blood: and I have given it to you upon the altar to make atonement for your souls: for it is the blood that maketh atonement by reason of the life."

Strictly, therefore, it is not the blood itself, but the *life* that is in it, which is regarded as making atonement. It may perhaps be said that the blood "was at once the most persuasive of gifts at God's altar, and the most potent purifier by which the sinner was purged of uncleanness and sin."[1] Again, it has been said, "No doubt the idea would arise that the 'soul'

[1] Article "Sacrifice" in Hastings' one volume *Dictionary of the Bible*, p. 817.

or life of an innocent animal involved in the blood was likely to be the more suitable and the more acceptable as an offering to God, as being the purest and most immaterial gift that could be offered to Him." [1] But possibly the reason why no better explanation is given is that the blood-shedding was regarded simply as a command of Jehovah that must be obeyed, but was not intended to be understood. In this case it is clear that the origin of the practice was thought to rest in God Himself, and not in man as trying to appease God.

But, while we cannot say with certainty what ideas about the efficacy of blood the Hebrew writers held, we can say with some assurance what they did *not* hold. They did not regard the sins of the worshipper as transferred to the victim,[2] nor the victim as being slain instead of the transgressor himself. This is important and the reasons for the statement should be carefully noted :

---

[1] *Encyclopædia of Religion and Ethics*, article " Expiation and Atonement," vol. v., p. 657.

[2] There are just two cases in which the transference of guilt or uncleanness is spoken of : the " living bird " of Lev. xiv. 53, which was supposed to carry away disease from a house ; and the goat " for Azazel " in Lev. xvi. 7–26, which was sent away to perish in the wilderness. (" Azazel " is probably the name of some demon of popular belief.) In both these cases, which appear to be very late, it seems that popular superstitions were taken up and used by Jewish legislators, as they were later by the Christian Church.

(1) Sins for which sacrifice made atonement were usually sins of ignorance or inadvertence, not those that deserved the penalty of death (Lev. iv.). For these latter no sacrifice was provided (Num. xv. 28–31).

(2) If the guilt of the worshipper had been regarded as transferred to the victim, the victim would then have been unclean, and no part of it could be eaten by priests or people.[1] Normally, it was so eaten.

(3) A meal offering, which required no sacrifice of life, was accepted from the poor.

Repentance and Amendment of Life

Remarkably little is said about this in connection with sacrifice. Partly, this may be due to the fact that many sacrifices were offered by the priests for the people collectively rather than individually. Not till Jeremiah and Ezekiel does the idea of individual responsibility clearly emerge.[2] Yet many offerings were made through the priests by individuals, in connection with their sins or " uncleannesses " ; and the absence of the note of penitence is strange.[3] This may

---

[1] This is clear from the account of the sacrifices on the Day of Atonement in Lev. xvi., especially verses 23–28. Even the persons who had touched these victims were unclean till they had bathed and washed their clothes.

[2] Jer. xxxi. 29, 30 ; Ezek. xviii. 1–4, etc.

[3] *Confession* is enjoined in Lev. v. 5, xvi. 21 ; Num. v. 7, etc.

be an additional reason for the prophetic denunciations of sacrifice. There was a constant tendency among the people to suppose that, if the sacrifices had been duly offered, all was well. Heathen and non-moral ideas were not entirely transcended, even by the priestly legislators : they rarely make, for example, any clear distinction between ritual uncleanness and real sin. And the popular ideas and practices were generally at a lower spiritual level than those of the written law.

The work for humanity that was done by the prophets, in proclaiming that it is moral righteousness alone which is desired by Jehovah, is quite priceless. It is due to the prophets much more than to the priests that the Hebrew nation achieved its vocation as a seed-bed for the Gospel. Without their work it would almost certainly have lapsed into heathenism and disappeared.

DIFFERING LEVELS IN THE IDEA OF SACRIFICE

We thus discern three main strata in the ideas of Sacrifice presented in the Old Testament.

(*a*) The pagan idea, largely non-moral, and usually associated with magic and superstition. God is regarded as unmoral, capricious, revengeful for offences which might be quite unintentional, one who is to be placated with offerings. Sacrifice here is literally a propitiation.

(*b*) The Hebrew priestly idea. Jehovah is a righteous God, in a covenant relation with Israel, a people that has agreed to serve Him in righteousness. Sacrifice is the perpetual renewal and reminder of the covenant between them. Sin is essentially disobedience, and can be " purged " with sacrifice so that the fellowship can be renewed. But non-moral ideas of sin were also entertained, and the failure to insist adequately on repentance made easy the lapse into heathen notions.

(*c*) The Hebrew prophetic idea. The prophets had a deeper sense than the priests of the righteous character of Jehovah, and of His moral requirements, such as the practice of justice between man and man. Sacrifice was " abomination " to Him if it did not carry with it surrender of the heart and obedience of life ; and it often appears to have been regarded by the prophets as worthless in any case. Repentance and amendment were vital. Sin grieved the loving heart of Jehovah (so especially Hosea and Jeremiah). There is no insistence on the need for ritual, except in Ezekiel and perhaps one or two others ; what Jehovah desires is the clean heart and the dedicated life. The " new covenant " which He designs to make with His people will be wholly inward and spiritual (Jer. xxxi. 31–34).

THE SERVANT OF JEHOVAH

There is one important group of prophecies
which stands out by itself—that concerned with
the " Servant of Jehovah." The group appears
in the later " Isaiah," and dates from the time
of the Exile, when Israel had suffered griev-
ously for his sins. There are four short sections,
viz. Isa. xlii. 1–4 ; xlix. 1–6 ; l. 4–9 ; and
lii. 13–liii. 12. Probably these sections form an
independent prophecy, by the unknown prophet
of Isa. xl.–lv., or another, which has been worked
into the main prophecy of Israel's restoration.

From Isa. xlix. 3 it seems clear that the
" Servant " is suffering and afflicted *Israel*
" Thou art my servant ; Israel, in whom I will be
glorified." This agrees with the use of the word
in the rest of the prophecy of restoration, where
the address, " Thou, Jacob, my servant," is of
frequent occurrence. But at times the word
seems to stand for the godly remnant who will
be the means of salvation for the rest (xlix. 5) ;
and who, beyond that, will bring light and salvation to the Gentiles (xlix. 6). The thought
reached by the prophet is that Israel has been
chosen not for his own sake, but for the world's
sake. Israel is despised, rejected, and well-nigh
martyred (l. 5, 6) ; but he will be raised up,
and his exaltation will " startle " (not " sprinkle ")

the nations (lii. 13–15). His sufferings will be discovered by them to have been vicarious and redemptive. The nations in amazement say of him, " Surely he hath borne our griefs and carried our sorrows ; the chastisement of our peace was upon him, and with his stripes we are healed " (liii. 4, 5).

The prophet does not explain *how* the suffering of Israel works redemption for the world at large, but this is certainly his meaning, and it is the profoundest thought reached in the Old Testament. It may have been suggested in part by the career of Jeremiah, who in Jer. xi. 19 says, " I was like a gentle lamb that is led to the slaughter," words taken up and used in Isa. liii. 7.

This prophecy is vital for our subject, because undoubtedly our Lord found in it the true picture of what his own redemptive work would be.[1] In this he appears to have been quite original ; there is no evidence that anyone before him had associated the Servant prophecy with the Messiah and his work. Nor was the Messianic expectation of the Jews in any way connected with their system of sacrifice. The Sadducees, who were the most devoted to the Temple ritual,

[1] Luke xxii. 37, " This which is written must be fulfilled in me, And he was reckoned with transgressors " (a quotation from Isa. liii. 12). The passage quoted in the synagogue at Nazareth (Luke iv. 16–19) beginning, " The Spirit of the Lord is upon me," is not one of the " Servant " sections, but would be closely associated with them in our Lord's mind.

had little expectation of, or use for, a Messiah. It was mainly the Pharisees and the Zealots who expected him to come, and (devoted though they were to the Law) their religion centred in the Synagogue rather than in the Temple. They never thought of the Messiah as a priest, as offering sacrifices, or as being sacrificed; they had no idea that he was to suffer or die. In their thoughts he was either a warrior king like Judas Maccabeus, or a supernatural " Son of Man " coming in the clouds of heaven. That was the main reason why they rejected Jesus, and why Jews still reject him.

But the disciples of Jesus, very soon after his resurrection, began to proclaim that he was the Messiah in spite of his apparent defeat and shameful and accursed death; and they grounded this assertion not alone on his victory over death, of which they claimed to be witnesses, but on the fulfilment of prophecy. They said it had been foretold that the Messiah should suffer, and it was mainly this prophecy they had in mind. Hence the fifty-third chapter of Isaiah has always expressed for the Christian mind what it felt to be the nature of Christ's redeeming work. He " fulfilled " the prophecy in a way the unknown prophet of the Exile had no idea of. He *was* the ideal Israel, the consummation and expression of what Israel had been raised up to be and to do for the world, and what the loyal remnant typified by Jeremiah had in part done.

We find then in the Old Testament that the Hebrew nation was Divinely trained in mind and heart for the coming and work of Christ along two main lines. First, there was the purification of the idea of Sacrifice : as a practice intended not to appease God, but to remove the sin which blocked the way to communion with Him, and to keep alive the sense of the covenant, of God's holiness, and of His moral demands. Secondly, there was the work of the prophets, who strove still further to purify the sacrificial system of its heathen elements, and to make clear that the only sacrifice really acceptable was that of the self to God. These two lines of preparation remained distinct from one another, and seemed often in sharp opposition.

Prophecy culminates in the ideal of the suffering Servant of Jehovah, who perhaps unites what was truest in both conceptions. The last three verses of Isa. liii. are badly corrupt (as may be seen from the number of marginal readings), and we cannot be at all sure what exactly was originally written. But if it was anything like the present Hebrew text, the Servant's " soul " (or life) is said to have been made " an offering for sin." This, if it was really the prophet's meaning, unites the two lines of preparation.

Whether this is so or not, this great prophecy does not, any more than do the Jewish sacrifices, teach vicarious *punishment*. What it does teach is vicarious and redemptive *suffering*, like that of Jeremiah and other prophets who were persecuted and martyred by those they sought to save, who did really save the nation from final apostasy and destruction, and who therefore helped in the salvation of the world.[1]

Vicarious suffering is woven deeply into the fabric of human life, and often it is, or may be, redemptive. A pure mother suffers agonies on behalf of her wayward son, and, when once he realises what his wild life has cost her, nothing may so move him to repentance as her suffering for him. It is along such lines as this that we must seek the real explanation of the vicarious suffering of Christ, who alone "fulfils" the deepest meaning of this great prophecy.

---

[1] It may perhaps be objected that I have done less than justice to such expressions as occur in verses 5, 6, 10 : " the chastisement of our peace was upon him, and with his stripes we are healed "; " the Lord hath laid on him the iniquity of us all "; " it pleased the Lord to bruise him." After very careful consideration, these passages do not seem to me to indicate that the prophet regarded the sufferings of the Servant as Divine punishment due to the heathen (or the disloyal part of Israel), but transferred to him. It is rather that his sufferings were discovered to have been voluntarily endured for the healing of others. " Sacrificial phraseology is here employed symbolically, to express the atoning or reconciling influence of the voluntary self-sacrifice of the loyal Israelites " (Workman, *The Servant of Jehovah*, p. 210).

CHAPTER III

ATONEMENT IN THE NEW TESTAMENT

WE have seen that the education of the Hebrew people, and its preparation, under Divine influences, to be the seed-bed for the Gospel of Christ, went on along two main lines, the priestly and the prophetic. The latter was much more ethical and spiritual than the former, and it developed the Messianic hope, which appears to have had no connection with the system of sacrifice to which the priests were devoted; though its crown, the prophecy of the Servant, which Jesus was the first to interpret as Messianic, possibly includes both conceptions. One striking difference between them was that the sacrificial system *did not look forward*, as prophecy undoubtedly did. While the primary work of the prophets was not foretelling the future, but rather the declaration of the mind and will of Jehovah in relation to contemporary issues, prophecy continually envisaged a coming Kingdom of God, in which His sovereignty should be established over the nation, and through Israel over the whole earth. There is no hint in the Old Testa-

4

ment (and there are hardly any in the New, even in the Epistle to the Hebrews, as we shall see [1]) that the sacrifices were thought of as " types " of something to come.

THE PROPHETIC MOVEMENT CARRIED FURTHER BY JESUS

In the days when the New Testament begins, the priestly system was being maintained in full vigour under the Sadducees at Jerusalem. The prophetic religion had shrivelled to Pharisaism, and had become in large measure legal, hard, and cold. Yet John the Baptist, and Jesus himself, were in the full line of the prophetic succession. There is no indication that John the Baptist ever insisted on sacrifice ; he called the people to repentance and the life of practical righteousness, just as the earlier prophets had done. And Jesus never, till close to the end of his life on earth, speaks of his work for men in sacrificial terms. Indeed, with the exception of the two occasions on which he directs healed lepers to go and offer the usual sacrifices (Mark i. 44 and Luke xvii. 14), he scarcely alludes to sacrifice at all. He twice quotes with full approval the declaration in Hosea, " I will have mercy and not sacrifice " (Hos. vi. 6 ; Matt. ix. 13 and xii. 7). He follows up the prophetic denunciations of sacrifice

[1] See below, p. 71.

by turning the money-changers, with the sheep
and oxen, out of the Temple precincts (Mark xi.
15-18). He proclaims the free forgiveness of
sins, as in the parables of the prodigal son and
of the Pharisee and the publican in the Temple,
and never once hints that God cannot forgive
unless a sacrifice is provided. He does indeed
lay down a condition of forgiveness, but this
is wholly inward—it is that we forgive those
who have offended us (Matt. vi. 14, 15;
Mark. xi. 25). He never suggests that there is
any obstacle to forgiveness on the side of God.
This is of vital importance to our subject, yet it
is hardly recognised by those who plead for the
Substitutionary view of the Atonement.

In studying the New Testament, while we
shall look in vain for any fully thought-out theory,
we must recognise that there was a development of ideas concerning the nature of Christ's
work of salvation. The scattered hints we find
in the Synoptic Gospels are different from the
more developed conceptions expressed in Paul's
letters to the Churches, and these again differ
from those we find in the Epistle to the Hebrews
and from those in the Johannine writings. The
saving work of Christ is looked at in different
ways, and from various points of view, and we
must try to get a sight of each main line of
interpretation.

We should also note that the subject is not

presented to us in a list of " doctrines," like
Incarnation, Atonement, Justification, Sanctification, as if each were intelligible by itself. The
work of Christ is rather regarded as a whole,
as depending on what he was and what he
revealed of God, of man, of sin, and of salvation ;
and we are apt to go wrong when we single out
some single aspect for separate treatment. Yet,
since no other course is open to us in this study,
we shall have to adopt it, bearing in mind its
dangers.

THE SYNOPTIC GOSPELS

Although the letters of Paul and probably
some other New Testament writings, like the
first epistle of Peter, appeared considerably earlier
than the first three Gospels, it is necessary to
deal with these in the first instance—because
they give us the background of information
without which the Epistles are not intelligible.
They are written from the point of view of the
impression which Jesus made on his contem-
poraries ; and, while the writers certainly held
the doctrine about him which the Church had
reached during the later decades of the first
century, they do not obtrude this doctrine, but
in the main they simply record what they believe
to be the facts, leaving these to make their own
impression.

It has already been stated that in the Gospels

Jesus never, till close to the end of his career on earth, speaks of sacrifice or atonement in connection with the forgiveness of sins by God. Forgiveness is always *free*, as was that of the prodigal's father. If this parable stood alone, it might be urged that in it (as is usual with Jesus) only one side of the truth is presented. But it does not. There is the companion parable of the Pharisee and the publican (Luke xviii. 9–14) ; and on several occasions Jesus tells people that their sins are forgiven, as in Mark ii. 5 and Luke vii. 47–50. The thought of God's Fatherhood rules and inspires everything that Jesus says about sin and forgiveness. Not only is the Father ever ready to welcome back the sinner, the moment he turns to Him in true repentance ; God takes the initiative Himself, and goes out to induce the sinner to return (Luke xv. 3–7).

In our earliest Gospel (that of Mark) Jesus says very little till near the end about his death ; [1] no doubt because the minds of the disciples were quite unable to entertain such an idea. Probably he had himself seen, at least from the time of the Temptation in the wilderness, that the course he was called to take could only end in one way. He felt himself to be the Messiah, but a Messiah of the Servant type, and not such as his con-

[1] There is a possible exception in the words about the Bridegroom in Mark ii. 20.

temporaries were looking for. But as soon as he has received Peter's confession, "Thou art the Christ" (Mark viii. 29–31), he begins at once to tell his disciples that he is to die. The solemn warning is repeated in Mark ix. 30–32 and x. 32–34, but it falls on deaf ears; they cannot think of a defeated Messiah.

Nowhere is it recorded that Jesus explained clearly to his disciples the meaning and purpose of the death which he knew was coming. Probably it would have been useless to attempt an explanation, even if (which perhaps is doubtful) he himself certainly knew it.[1] At the same time, we may well believe that many things he said to them have not been recorded because at the time they were not understood. Only in two passages is there any hint of an explanation.

The first is Mark x. 45 and its parallel in Matt. xx. 28: "For verily the Son of man came not to be ministered unto, but to minister, and to give (that is, to part with) his life as ransom for many."

This arises out of the request of James and John for the best places in the Kingdom, and the point of it is that he who would be greatest must serve the most and be willing to take the lowest place.

[1] Note the prayer in the garden, "If it be possible, let this cup pass away from me" (Matt. xxvi. 39).

The second passage is Mark xiv. 24 (= Matt. xxvi. 28), and follows the handing of the cup to the disciples at the last supper :

" This is my blood of the covenant, which is shed for many " (Matthew adds " for the forgiveness of sins," but this is very probably a later addition to the saying).[1]

We note in both passages the use of the word " many." This is almost certainly an echo of Isa. liii. 11, 12 : " by his knowledge shall my righteous Servant justify many " ; " yet he bare the sin of many " ; and it shows that the Servant prophecy was in the mind of Jesus. Let us try to catch the essential ideas that are here in part expressed. The thoughts of Jesus are full of the coming of the Kingdom, as is clear from Mark xiv. 25, " I will no more drink of the fruit of the vine until that day when I drink it new in the kingdom of God." He sees clearly now that the Kingdom will not come without his death. For him that Kingdom was no Government system, but a Love system, in which God was not to be called King, but Father, and in which men were to be brothers one to another.

---

[1] I take these passages as they stand, believing them to represent substantially authentic sayings of Jesus. I am not convinced by Dr. Rashdall's elaborate argument (in *The Idea of Atonement in Christian Theology*, pp. 29–39) that " they are of exactly the kind which are spoken of by critics as ecclesiastical additions."

The one obstacle to its coming was human sin, especially the hardness and blindness of men; and the way could only be cleared as this obstacle was removed. A "ransom" is money paid for the release of captives. Here the price is clearly his life, and the captivity is that of sin. The death of Jesus will work deliverance or redemption: it will set the captives free, remove the obstacle, and so bring in the Kingdom. No more than this is explained; it is futile to ask prosaic questions such as "to whom was the price paid?" or "how precisely was the deliverance to be effected?" In these closing days and hours of human intercourse with his disciples, Jesus is not trying to teach them speculative theology, but to nerve them to keep their faith in him in spite of his death; for he sees that unless he can do this his work will be in vain—the task given him will be impossible of achievement.

The other expression, "the blood of the covenant," has obviously a sacrificial meaning, and it is the only one in which Jesus speaks of his death in these terms. Probably we must connect it with Ex. xxiv. 5–8, where Moses, after sprinkling the blood of the victims on the people, says, "Behold the blood of the covenant which Jehovah hath made with you." The ceremony, as we saw in the last chapter,[1] would

[1] See above, p. 37.

assure the people of acceptance and communion with Jehovah, and would solemnly renew their compact with Him. But we should also notice Paul's account of the last supper in 1 Cor. xi. 25, where he represents Jesus as saying, " This cup is the *new* covenant in my blood." (Some MSS. have also inserted the word "new" before "covenant" in Mark and Matthew). The allusion would seem to be to Jeremiah's prophecy of the "new covenant" written on the hearts of men (Jer. xxxi. 31), where there is nothing to suggest an outward sacrifice.

On the whole, we may probably take it that this was our Lord's crowning act in the course of preparing his disciples to face his death. He assures them by this beautiful and solemn ceremony that his death will be the greatest and final means of getting rid of the obstacle which sin puts in the way of the coming of the Kingdom,[1] of assuring men of God's forgiveness, and establishing His "new covenant" in their hearts. There is no suggestion, here or anywhere else in the Gospels, that Jesus endures the Divine wrath, or suffers punishment for human sin. While we find terrible warnings of the consequences of persisting in sin, especially when this is done

[1] Note Paul's addition in 1 Cor. xi. 26, " For as oft as ye eat this bread, and drink this cup, ye proclaim the Lord's death *till he come.*" The "Coming" in his thoughts meant the establishment of the Kingdom.

wilfully against the light of God's Spirit in the heart (as in Mark iii. 28-30), there is no hint of any "transference" of guilt or punishment.

Before leaving the Synoptic Gospels, we should note the very large space they all devote to the circumstances leading up to and attending the death of Christ, and the prominence they give to the agony in the garden, and the sense of desolation on the Cross. (In Mark's Gospel chapters x. to xv. are more than one-third of the whole book.) Evidently they all felt the Crucifixion to be of supreme importance, though they leave it to make its own impression, and never attempt to explain it. This is, I think, a point that should be borne in mind by those who are inclined to think of the death of Jesus as nothing more than a martyrdom.[1] The Gospels certainly suggest that it had a deeper meaning. It is true that Divine forgiveness follows at once on true repentance ; for God, being Father, is already reconciled to men ; it is also true that, in Dr. Rashdall's words, "He in whom the sinful will has been changed, and in proportion as it has been changed, is already reconciled to God." But the change in the sinful will is a harder thing than some imagine it to be. "How

[1] As Dr. Rashdall does in the work alluded to above. For the quotation that follows, see p. 49.

hardly," says Jesus, " shall they that have riches enter into the kingdom of God " (Mark x. 23). To the question of his amazed disciples, " Then who can be saved ? " Jesus replies, " With men it is impossible, but not with God, for with God all things are possible "—not by the use of force or compulsion, but by winning men's wills through perfect love. The Gospels suggest to us the spiritual dynamic which the Divine Love was holding in reserve, and which the Cross revealed.

THE ACTS OF THE APOSTLES

This book professes to give an account of the earliest preaching of Christianity ; and the Atonement, at least explicitly, hardly appears in it at all. There is the message of "repentance and remission of sins," as in ii. 38, but there is very little about the death of Jesus in this connection. When his death is mentioned, this is usually as incidental to his *resurrection,* which receives all the emphasis. Salvation is offered to those who accept Jesus as the Son of God, that is, as the Messiah—which was the supreme difficulty with the Jews, for how could a crucified criminal be the Messiah ? The answer of the Apostles is twofold : first that God has raised him from the dead, and of that they themselves are witnesses (ii. 32) ; and, second, that it was foretold in prophecy that the Messiah should suffer and die. " Him, being delivered up by the determinate counsel and foreknowledge of God, ye by the hand of lawless men did crucify and slay ; whom God raised up " (ii. 23–24). It is the Servant prophecy that Peter has in mind, as is seen by the frequency with which he calls Jesus the " Servant " of God.[1]

Only in one passage in Acts is the language of Atonement used, viz. xx. 28 : " Take heed therefore to yourselves," Paul says to the Ephesian elders, " and to all the flock in which the Holy Spirit placed you as bishops (or overseers), to shepherd the church of God, which he won for a possession through his own blood." [2]

Such an expression as " through his own blood " is hardly found elsewhere in the New Testament applied to God, but no doubt the meaning is " in the person of His Son." The thought is that, as Christ gave his life for the Church, its leaders ought to give it their best service. Paul is using the sacrifice of Christ as an argument and a motive for self-sacrifice in Christians, as is his custom. He is appealing to a well-recognised fact, the theological signifi-

[1] So correctly translated in the R.V. : see Acts iii. 13, 26 ; iv. 27, 30. Typical passages in Acts are : iii. 18 ; v. 30–32 ; x. 43 ; xiii. 38, 39 ; and xxvi. 18. (In the last it is the risen Jesus who is speaking to Paul.)

[2] It is interesting to note that the same language is used in the Epistle to the Ephesians in i. 14 : " the redemption of the possession."

cance of which it was no part of his purpose to explain.[1]

THE PAULINE EPISTLES

It is not easy, and perhaps it is not very profitable, to separate out Paul's expressions about Atonement in the restricted sense. His whole soul is full of what Christ has done and is doing for men, and he does not think in doctrines. His letters fall into three main chronological groups :

(1) 1 (and probably 2) Thessalonians, about A.D. 52.

(2) Galatians, Romans, and 1 and 2 Corinthians, about 57–59.

(3) Colossians, Philemon, Ephesians, and Philippians, written from prison at Rome about 62.[2]

[1] It may be well at this point to make one remark in regard to Dr. Rashdall's argument (*The Idea of the Atonement*, pp. 70–73 and 75–83), that the whole of the sacrificial language found in the New Testament concerning the suffering of Christ can be explained if the first Christian leaders, within a very few years (or even months) of his death, identified him with the Servant of Isa. liii. This they no doubt did, as we have seen ; but, being what they were, would they ever had the insight to make that identification if Jesus had not led the way ? I cannot think they would ; and therefore I incline to attach a good deal more importance and authority to the language they use than Dr. Rashdall does. The Gospels themselves indicate that they looked on the death of their Master as much more than a martyrdom ; and I do not think their views about it can be lightly set aside as mistaken.

[2] The Pastoral Epistles, 1 and 2 Timothy and Titus, appear

In these letters there are about thirty passages which bear more or less on Christ's death in relation to human salvation. A certain development can be traced in the writer's expressions as we advance from his earliest to his later letters. Perhaps his thoughts can be broadly summarised somewhat as follows :—

(1) "*The Wrath of God.*" This expression appears mainly in 1 and 2 Thessalonians and in Romans. In 1 Thess. v. 9, 10 we read, "For God appointed us not to wrath, but unto the obtaining of salvation through our Lord Jesus Christ, who died for us, that, whether we wake or sleep, we should live together with him." In 2 Thess. i. 6–10 the writer looks forward to "the revelation of the Lord Jesus from heaven, with the angels of his power in flaming fire, rendering vengeance to them that know not God." We must bear in mind that this was a familiar Messianic conception. One of the chief functions of the Messiah, as popularly conceived, was to "judge" the world, setting up God's people and destroying their adversaries. In Rom. ii. 5–11 Paul corrects the common idea that it is the Jews who will be saved and the Gentiles who will be visited with "wrath," by showing that "there is no respect of persons

to be, in the main at least, a good deal later than Paul's time. There may be some genuine Pauline fragments in 2 Timothy.

with God," and that for Jew and Gentile alike it is only righteousness that will avail. The idea of "wrath" is an *eschatological* one, included in that of the coming of the Messiah to judgment; it is in Paul's earliest letters that it receives the chief emphasis; and, as his life advanced, it appears to have receded into the background of his mind.[1] Only in 1 Thess. i. 10 and Rom. v. 9 is Christ said to "deliver (or save) us from wrath." In the latter passage the Greek has "the wrath" simply, which suggests that Paul then thought of it as a process of judgment which worked itself out in men's experience, rather than as an arbitrary Divine sentence.[2]

(2) What Christ by his death delivers us from is *Sin*, which is called by different names. In Gal. i. 4 he has delivered us "out of this present evil world"; in Col. i. 13 he "delivered us out of the power of darkness"; in Rom. vii. 24, 25 Paul thanks God through Jesus Christ for deliverance "from the body of this death." He glories in "the cross of our Lord Jesus Christ, through which the world hath been crucified unto me, and I unto the world" (Gal. vi. 14). "Christ

---

[1] How far had Jesus himself held the popular conception of "judgment"? Very significant is his action in the synagogue at Nazareth, when reading from Isa. lxi. he closes the book and does not read the words "and the day of vengeance of our God." Compare John xii. 47, "I came not to judge the world, but to save the world."

[2] So Dodd, *The Meaning of Paul for To-day*, pp. 62–65.

crucified," though " to the Jews a stumbling-block and to Gentiles foolishness, is to them that are called, both Jews and Greeks, Christ the power of God and the wisdom of God " (1 Cor. i. 23, 24). The law is unable to work this deliverance (Rom. viii. 3, 4), but God does it by " sending His Son in the likeness of sinful flesh and as an offering for sin." Hence it would be "madness" for the Galatians to turn back to the law (Gal. iii. 1). The Cross of Christ works *a moral change in men*, a thing which it was wholly beyond the power of the law to accomplish.

(3) Christ by his death *reconciles us to God* (Rom. v. 6–11). Not once does Paul speak of God being reconciled to us by Christ—it would seem that he has taken care to avoid such an expression. The clearest of all the reconciliation passages is perhaps 2 Cor. v. 18–20 : " All things are of God, who reconciled us to Himself through Christ, and gave unto us (Apostles) the ministry of reconciliation : to wit, that God was in Christ, reconciling the world unto himself, not reckoning unto them their trespasses, and having committed unto us the word of reconciliation." He says, " *All things are of God* " : the whole process of reconciliation starts with God, and not with anything that we can do to gain His favour. Not even the death of Christ procures His for-

giving love, for this is ours from the beginning. In Eph. ii. 13–16 the Gentiles are "made nigh in the blood of Christ," which reconciles Jews and Gentiles to one another because it reconciles them to God, breaking down "the middle wall of partition" set up by the Jewish law, and thus "slaying the enmity" between them.

(4) This reconciliation Christ effects *by uniting us with himself*. This thought of "mystical union" is Paul's deepest and most characteristic contribution to the doctrine of Atonement. Christ died—therefore, united with him, we *all* die to sin (2 Cor. v. 14). Christ rose from the dead—therefore, united with him, we *all* rise into a new moral life (2 Cor. v. 15).[1] "Him who knew no sin he made to be sin on our behalf, that we might become the righteousness of God in him" (2 Cor. v. 21) ; a passage which we may perhaps paraphrase thus : "He, though sinless, was made one with us in our sinfulness, that we, though sinful, might be made one with him in his righteousness." Christ's death and resurrection are, as it were, all in one piece, and we have to unite ourselves with him in both. The power by which we do this is what Paul calls "faith."

Christ is thus regarded by Paul as not so much *another person* as the head of the whole race,

[1] Other characteristic passages are Gal. ii. 19–21 ; Rom. vi. 4–11 ; 2 Cor. iv. 10, etc.

the "second Adam." What he does, the whole race does in him, so far as it is united to him by faith (1 Cor. xv. 21, 22).

(5) It is in the light of this deep sense of "mystical union" with Christ that we must explain Paul's use of sacrificial language—which only occurs twice or thrice in all his writings. As has been well said, we cannot properly understand Paul's Evangelicalism unless we first understand his Mysticism. In the order of our thought, Rom. vi. should precede Rom. iii.[1]

The chief passage claiming attention is Rom. iii. 21–26, and it is a very difficult one to interpret with certainty. Paul is bringing into contrast with the righteousness of the law the "righteousness of God" which is through faith in Christ :

" Whom God set forth as propitiatory, through faith, by his blood, to show his righteousness, because of the passing over of the sins done aforetime, in the forbearance of God ; for the showing, I say, of his righteousness at this present season, that he might himself be just, and the justifier of him that hath faith in Jesus."

The noun " propitiation " is used in our

---

[1] For Paul's readers this may have been otherwise. As Professor C. R. Dodd says, " to the ancients it seemed that they had told the inmost secret of a matter when they had expressed it in terms of sacrifice, whereas for us it is just there that the difficulty begins " (*The Meaning of Paul*, p 97).

Version, but as the word is here the adjective *hilasterion*, it is better to translate it " propitiatory," as in the margin of the R.V. It is obvious that the word is not used in its ordinary pagan sense of soothing an angry deity, because the offering comes not from man but from God, who has " *set forth* " Christ as propitiatory. Whatever exactly Paul means by the phrase " by his blood," it is clear that he was not falling back into pagan ideas of propitiation. The purpose of God in the sacrifice of Christ, stated twice over, is " to manifest his righteousness "— which must mean to reveal His character by getting rid of sin. Christ is " propitiatory " because he by his death *does* get rid of it, as the Jewish sacrifices were supposed to do. The old word is taken up, as often by Christian teachers, and given a new and deeper meaning. *Because* God is righteous He takes means to set men right with Him, in order that they may become righteous too.[1]

Other sacrificial passages are I Cor. x. 16, 17, and xi. 23–27, where Paul deals with the " cup " and " bread " of the Lord's Supper, as showing

---

[1] This certainly seems to be the true meaning of the latter part of verse 26. There can be no conflict in the Divine nature between " justice " and the desire to " justify " sinners ; and apart from certain theological theories the verse could never have been so interpreted. It should be remembered that " just " and " righteous " are the same word in Greek (*dikaios*).

forth the "communion" of the blood and body
of Christ—just as other sacrifices were supposed
to establish communion with the Divine. There
is also 1 Cor. v. 7, "For our passover also hath
been sacrificed, even Christ"—suggested by the
thought of the need of "purging out the old
leaven" of impurity—a passage which shows
how early the conception had taken hold that
the paschal lamb was in some sense a symbol
of Christ.[1] It should be remembered that the
paschal lamb was not an offering *for sin*, but
a memorial of the deliverance from Egypt
(Exod. xii. 14).

We have one passage in which Christ is said
to have become a "*curse*" for us, Gal. iii. 13 :
"Christ redeemed us from the curse of the law,
having become a curse for us ; for it is written,
Cursed is every one that hangeth on a tree."
This is a purely "Rabbinical" argument, and
the circle of ideas which it represents is so different from ours that there is difficulty in catching
its meaning. A "curse" was supposed to work
itself out automatically. Christ has absorbed
into himself in his crucifixion, and exhausted,
the whole venom of the ancient curse pronounced
on breakers of the law. He has triumphed over

---

[1] This and possibly the "Lamb of God" in John seem to
be the only expressions in the New Testament suggesting that
the Jewish sacrifices were "types" of something to come.

it, and the curse is no longer to be feared.[1]
Paul apparently throws out this argument by
the way, as something that has occurred to him
and should have weight with Jews. He does
not follow it up.

The upshot of Paul's thoughts about the
redeeming significance of the death of Christ is,
then, that he died as our representative (not as
our substitute), in order that we might die with
him (to sin), and live with him (to righteousness).

"In the theology of Paul, it is not the death conceived
by itself alone that has redemptive significance, but the
death as part of the entire process of the Divine self-
identification with humanity, which makes it possible for
believers here and now to become partakers of the Divine
life of Christ, and so sharers in his triumph and resurrection. To Paul, Christ is not only the passive sufferer,
he is the conquering Lord; and the benefits of his
sufferings and his conquest are mediated to his disciples
by the mystic union with him which is brought about
by faith."[2]

[1] See Dodd, *The Meaning of Paul*, pp. 101, 102.
[2] *Encyclopædia of Religion and Ethics*, article "Expiation
and Atonement," vol. v. p. 642.

CHAPTER IV

ATONEMENT IN THE NEW TESTAMENT
(*continued*)

THE EPISTLE TO THE HEBREWS

THIS book is of great importance for our subject, being the only one in the New Testament that treats the Atonement throughout on sacrificial lines, the only one that calls Christ a Priest, the only one that systematically represents the Jewish sacrifices as shadows of a reality greater than themselves. The book had a hard fight to get into our New Testament at all, and it succeeded, apparently, only because of the belief, uncritical and quite clearly erroneous, that it was written by Paul. The real author is unknown. The most attractive suggestion is that of Harnack, that it was written by Priscilla, with the help of her husband Aquila. It is certainly first-century work, for it is quoted without acknowledgment by Clement of Rome, in his letter to the Corinthian

Church, about A.D. 95. It seems to have been addressed to some community consisting mainly of Jewish Christians, perhaps at Rome, who were in danger, under the stress of persecution, of falling back into Judaism.

The whole point of the letter, or sermon, is that, if they do this, they will be forsaking the substance for the shadow, the eternal for the perishable, the reality for mere appearance. The writer starts from the standpoint of the Alexandrian philosophy of Philo, drawn ultimately from Plato—a philosophy which sees in temporal things a mere shadow or copy of eternal or heavenly realities. He (or she) applies this idea to the Jewish law, to show that its ceremonies and sacrifices belong to the order of weak and passing shadows, while Christ is strong, substantial and eternal.[1] He nowhere suggests that the ceremonies were instituted as "types," to hint, by a kind of riddle, at something that should come in the future. He sees clearly that they did not look forward ; whatever efficacy they had was purely for the time.

It is his treatment of the death of Christ that we have to study. At the outset (i. 3) he speaks of Christ as having "made purification for sins"

[1] This is clearest in ch. viii. 5, where the writer says that the priests "serve that which is a copy and shadow of the heavenly things." Compare vii. 18, 19, and The Wisdom of Solomon, ix. 8.

(as the old sacrifices were thought to do) ; and in ch. ii. 9 of his winning " glory and honour " by "tasting death for[1] every man." In ch. ii. 17 Christ is the High Priest who "makes propitiation for the sins of the people." The Greek words are *hilaskesthai tas hamartias* : Christ (as in the Old Testament) is spoken of, not as propitiating God, but as removing sins out of His sight.

The thought of Christ as High Priest (the *real* Priest, though fully and completely human— ch. ii. 10–17) is expanded in chapters v–x. In ch. v.–vii. he is the " priest after the order of Melchizedek "—that is, not one appointed by a " carnal commandment " (vii. 16), by any outward and temporary law, as Aaron was, but in the eternal nature of things—a priest, as we might say, "after the order of humanity." In the ninth chapter details of the " first covenant " are given, and it is shown that the sacrifices could only yield a *ceremonial* cleanness, not a real one. The true priest's work is said to be (verse 26) " *to put away sin* by the sacrifice of himself." The blood of Christ " shall *cleanse your conscience from dead works to serve the living God* " (verse 14). This thought is carried further in chapter x, where we are said to be " *sanctified* through the

---

[1] The preposition used here, and most often in the New Testament, is *huper* (not *anti*), which does not mean " instead of."

offering of the body of Jesus Christ once for all "
(verse 10, compare verses 22, 29 and xiii. 12)—
so that we can now enter the holy place with
boldness (verse 19), and are not kept off by fear
as before. It is *real* righteousness, not ceremonial
and not fictitious, that Christ by his death works
in us.

All outward sacrifices have now been done away
in Christ ; the only sacrifice that remains for
Christians to render is that of the self (x. 8, 9),
with praise and the unselfish life (xiii. 15, 16).
The book, rightly understood, is a powerful argument, especially to Jews, and it springs out of the
abounding spiritual life of the first century. It
would have been a profound loss had it been
excluded from the New Testament. It contains,
however, no trace of Paul's characteristic mysticism ; and its expressions about God as " a con-
suming fire " (xii. 29), and one into whose hands
" it is a terrible thing to fall " (x. 31), hardly
suggest the tender thought of Fatherhood that
we find, for instance, in the Johannine writings.
There is nothing here quite on the spiritual level
of " he that hath seen me hath seen the Father,"
or " we love because he first loved us."

THE FIRST EPISTLE OF PETER

This " catholic " or general letter was, like the
Epistle to the Hebrews, addressed to Christians

suffering from persecution or the threat of it, and the writer appeals to Christ's patient endurance of suffering as an encouragement to bear it bravely (ch. ii. 21–24 ; iv. 1, 13, etc.). The letter is largely Pauline in tone and method, but there is good evidence for Petrine authority. The writer says (v. 12) that he employed Silvanus as his amanuensis, and the wording may be due in part to the latter. Here also, as in Hebrews, we note the absence of the Pauline mysticism ; but there is the same strong ethical feeling. Christ's death is spoken of as delivering us from sin, and bringing us real holiness. In ch. i. 2 the " sprinkling of the blood of Jesus Christ " is, together with " obedience," said to be the outcome of " sanctification of the Spirit." (On the ordinary view, the " sprinkling " should have come first.) In ch. i. 18, 19 redemption is said to be, not from punishment, but from a " vain manner of life." In ii. 24 it is stated that Christ " bare our sins in His own body on the tree, *that we having passed away from sins might live unto righteousness* " ; and in iii. 18 that " Christ also suffered for sins once, the righteous for the unrighteous, that he might bring us to God." Christ is nowhere called a " priest," but Christians are to be " a holy priesthood, to offer up spiritual sacrifices, acceptable to God through Jesus Christ " (ii. 5). It is clear that, in the writer's mind, the whole purpose of the Atonement is to work a moral change in the hearts of men.[1]

The Johannine Writings: (a) The Fourth Gospel

The three principal books in the New Testament that are connected, either by tradition or by explicit statement, with the name of " John " are the fourth Gospel, the first Epistle, and the Apocalypse or Book of Revelation. The first two of these are almost certainly by the same author, but his identity is unknown. The Apocalypse, in which alone the author calls himself " John," can hardly have been written by the same person as the others, though he may have belonged to the same school of Christian thought. All the books belong, apparently, to the close of the first century.

In the fourth Gospel, as in the writings of Paul, the idea of Atonement is all bound up with the larger thought of Christ and his revelation of God, and cannot be properly understood alone.[2]

[1] I exclude from this survey of the New Testament writings the second Epistle attributed to Peter, which, together with the Pastoral Epistles, I cannot think to belong to the first century. Also James, Philemon, Jude, and 2 and 3 John, as containing little or nothing on the subject of Atonement.

[2] I have attempted to set forth the broad outlines of the Johannine teaching in my book *The Word Made Flesh*, chaps. iv, v, vii, and viii.

All that can be done here is to select the passages
that refer specially to the death of Christ in
relation to the salvation of men.

The first of these (apart from an expression
attributed to John the Baptist, which will be
mentioned later) is ch. iii. 14, 15 : " And as Moses
lifted up the serpent in the wilderness, even so
must the Son of man be lifted up ; that whoso-
ever believeth may in him have eternal life."
The " lifting up " of Jesus is mentioned again
in viii. 28 and xii. 32, 33, and it almost certainly
suggests a deeper thought of the *exaltation* of Christ,
behind that of the physical raising of his body
on the Cross. " It is not so much the death as
the *life* of Christ that has saving power." [1] Whatever may be its precise significance, there is clearly
in it no suggestion of a *sacrifice*.

In ch. vi. 51 Jesus is reported as saying, " The
bread which I will give is my flesh, for the life
of the world " ; and this is followed in verse 53
by the words, " Except ye eat the flesh of the
Son of man, and drink his blood, ye have not
life in yourselves." There is probably an allusion
here to the Eucharistic observance, but the
" eating " and " drinking " are wholly spiritual.
The life of Jesus is not only given *to* men, but

---

[1] *Encyclopædia of Religion and Ethics*, vol. v., p. 642. The
author of the fourth Gospel loved symbolism, and there is often
a deeper meaning in his words than appears on the surface.

sacrificed *for* them, and this life and death they must assimilate in their own experience.

In ch. x. 11 ff. Jesus speaks of himself as the "good (or beautiful) Shepherd," who gives his life on behalf of (*huper*, not *anti*) the sheep, as a voluntary sacrifice. Another significant passage is xii. 24, suggested by the coming of some Greeks with the desire to see Jesus: "Except a grain of wheat fall into the ground and die, it abideth by itself alone; but if it die, it beareth much fruit." The following verses show that Jesus is thinking not only of the general principle of "life through death," but specially of the dark pathway which he has himself to tread, the death through which alone his own life can bear fruit. "Now is my soul troubled, and what shall I say? Father, save me from this hour. But for this cause came I unto this hour." But the principle holds for others as well as for himself: "Where I am, there shall also my servant be."

In ch. xv. 13 Jesus says, "Greater love hath no man than this, that a man lay down his life for his friends"; and in xvii. 19, "For their sakes I consecrate myself (that is, devote myself to death), that they also may be consecrated in truth." Those, I believe, are all the passages in this Gospel in which Jesus is represented as speaking of the significance of his death.

Nowhere is he reported as using the language

of expiatory sacrifice. Yet the writer himself appears to have held some such view. He attributes to John the Baptist the saying, " Behold the Lamb of God which taketh away (or beareth) the sin of the world " (i. 29) [1] ; and twice in the first Epistle he uses the word " propitiation." In view of the freedom he allows himself to expand and interpret what he thought to be the deeper meaning of the sayings of Jesus, it is remarkable that he does not attribute to him any such expression.

It may be well to examine his thought a little more fully.   We note the allusions to the " glory " of Jesus in immediate connection with his death and the victory he would thereby win. In ch. vii. 39 the writer comments, " For the Spirit was not yet given, because Jesus was not yet glorified." In xiii. 31, immediately Judas leaves the company to betray him, Jesus says, " Now is the Son of man glorified, and God is glorified in him." The " glory " of which he speaks is to be found in absolute obedience, even to death, in the fulfilling, by perfect self-surrender, of the will of God. " I glorified thee on the earth by accomplishing the work which thou hast given me to do " (xvii. 4). When Jesus washes his

---

[1] Since the paschal lamb was not an offering for *sin* (see above, p. 68), it seems probable that the " lamb " of Isa. liii. 7 is what was in the writer's thought.

disciples' feet, he shows them that to win his true glory he must descend to the depths of what men call humiliation. (Compare Luke xxii. 27, "I am in the midst of you as he that serveth".) His humiliation even to death, and his true glory, are but different sides of the same reality. But the glory can only be achieved as the disciples share it: "I am glorified *in them*" (xvii. 10; compare verses 22 and 26); it is only as they "eat his flesh" that they can share his life. The glory of God, the fulfilment of His purpose, can only be reached as men have His character, which is the character of Jesus, reproduced in themselves. This is the high-water mark of the teaching of Redemption in the New Testament.

(b) THE FIRST EPISTLE OF JOHN

This "catholic" Epistle was probably issued by the same writer shortly after his Gospel appeared. It contains the same essential thoughts, but they are expressed more simply, and with less of symbolism. In ch. i. 7 he says, "If we walk in the light, we have fellowship one with another, and the blood of Jesus his Son cleanseth us from all sin." The "walking in the light" is the *condition* of knowing the inward "cleansing," which, the verb being in the present tense, is a process continually going on. At the same time it is through this continual cleansing that the

" light " can shine undimmed by our sinfulness.
In ch. i. 9 the sinfulness that needs removal must
be continually confessed and repented of. " If
we confess our sins, he is faithful and righteous
to forgive our sins, and to cleanse us from all un-
righteousness." The " righteousness " or " justice "
of God is not a quality in Him that compels
Him to condemn us ; it means that He is faithful
to His promise to pardon and restore those who
truly turn to Him.

In ch. ii. 2 and iv. 10 Christ is said to be the
" propitiation " (*hilasmos*) for our sins. The
meaning is the same as in Romans and Hebrews :
the " propitiation " comes from God, not from
us, and is the expression of His saving love
(iv. 9, 10). It is directed to the removal of our
sin. This love has been expressed in Christ, and
is to be reproduced in us (iv. 11–14). The thought
of our identification with Christ is latent here,
but is not explicitly drawn out. Love is the
supreme reality in the universe (" *God* is love,"
iv. 8, 16) ; and love must take possession of our
lives if we are to be at one with God.

(c) The Apocalypse

The minds of devout Jews, both before and
after the coming of Christ, turned, in times of
persecution and calamity, to the writing of Apocalypses, in which men were encouraged to bear it

with fortitude by the assurance that God was about to intervene and deliver them. This book is the greatest of many similar ones. They all endeavour to convey spiritual truth by veiling it in allegorical figures, often strange and fantastic. In this book the " Beast " is almost certainly the persecuting Roman State, and " Babylon " is Rome.

The humanity of Jesus is here well-nigh forgotten ; he is throughout a superhuman and glorified figure. And with the humanity of Jesus has disappeared also the Fatherhood of God. God is spoken of as the " Father " of Christ, but never as the Father of men. " We hear hoarse cries for the day of vengeance, and see the warrior Christ coming to deluge the earth with blood." [1] The book embodies Jewish anticipations of the " day of vengeance of our God," coloured and softened by Christian conceptions. Perhaps some previous and non-Christian apocalypses have been worked up by the writer, and adapted to the needs of his day. Like Hebrews, the book was with difficulty admitted to the Canon of the New Testament ; it was rejected by Luther, and never commented on by Calvin.

Sacrificial imagery is here abundant. Christ is " the Lamb that hath been slain " ; but he is

[1] Forbes, quoted by Moffatt, *Introduction to the Literature of the New Testament*, p. 511.

6

not a figure of submission as in Isa. liii ; he is also " the Lion " (v. 5), and full of wrath (vi. 16). In i. 5 praise is given " to him that loveth us, and loosed [1] us from our sins in his own blood." In v. 9 the prayer is, " Thou wast slain and didst purchase unto God with thy blood men of every tribe," etc. In vii. 14 the " great multitude " before the throne is said to consist of those who " washed their robes and made them white in the blood of the Lamb " ; and in xii. 11 Michael and his angels overcome the dragon " because of the blood of the Lamb." These are the familiar expressions of the Book of Revelation, and they carry the meaning which sacrifice bore to devout Jews generally. Christ by his death has removed human sin from the sight of God, as in Jewish thought the sacrifices did. It is nowhere suggested that he appeased the wrath of God. He is the supreme and perfect sacrifice, interpreted precisely in accordance with Jewish conceptions.

SUMMARY OF THE NEW TESTAMENT TEACHING

If now we try to put before our minds the broader features of the New Testament teaching about Atonement, we shall find that principles such as these are dominant :

[1] This is the R.V., which reads *lusanti* with the best MSS. The text of the A.V. has *lousanti*, " washed."

(1) Everything starts from the revelation of God as Father, who has expressed His character and His saving love in the person and work of Jesus Christ His Son.

(2) It is from this heart of love that human salvation springs. It is not wrought by anything we can bring to God, but by what He gives to us. Atonement is always man's reconciliation to God, never His reconciliation to men.

(3) Redemption is always deliverance from sin, and the purpose of the Atonement is in the first instance not to deliver us from punishment, but to bring us to God and enable us to live the life of righteousness as His sons. Deliverance from hell is purely incidental to this.

(4) Nowhere is Christ said to have been punished in our stead, or to have endured the wrath of God. (The nearest approach to such an expression is in Gal. iii. 13, which has been dealt with above).[1]

(5) The deepest thought reached is that of Paul and " John," that Christ makes himself one with us, in order that we may unite ourselves to him by faith—" dying with him " to sin, in order that his righteousness may become ours because his life is actually reproduced in us. There is no such thing as a fictitious or make-believe righteousness. God does not " impute "

[1] See above, pp. 68, 69.

to us anything that is not already there, at least in germ and possibility.

There is one passage in the Book of Revelation which, if it is rightly translated, is very note-worthy. If it is not, it seems at any rate to convey a deep truth that is in accordance with the thoughts of Christ which, in the course of the first century, the great Christian teachers came to hold.

" And all that dwell on the earth shall worship him, everyone whose name hath not been written in the book of life of *the Lamb slain from the foundation of the world* " (Rev. xiii. 8).[1]

Whether or not this is the real meaning of the particular passage, the thought it suggests is helpful and true : that the historic Sacrifice of Christ on Calvary was the supreme manifestation in time of something that had been from all eternity in the very nature of God Himself : that all through human history He had been taking our sin upon Himself, enduring it and forgiving it. The Cross was the highest revelation of God's eternal attitude in relation to human sin.

WAS THE CROSS PREDETERMINED ?

There is one difficulty in the New Testament teaching on this subject that should perhaps

[1] If we compare this passage with Rev. xvii. 8, we cannot be sure that the words " from the foundation of the world " do not belong to " written in the book of life," in which case the translation will be as in the R.V. margin.

receive brief notice. It is suggested (for example in Acts ii. 23, " being delivered up by the determinate counsel and foreknowledge of God ") that the death of Christ was predetermined and so had to be. We are apt to infer from this that anyone who so thinks of it must regard the men who brought about the death of Jesus as not free agents, and therefore not to blame. But the writers of the New Testament certainly did not draw this inference. In the passage quoted Peter goes on to say, " Ye *by the hands of lawless men* did crucify and slay." These writers habitually spoke of what they regarded as the fulfilment of prophecy as if it were something that must happen anyway. Certain events occurred, they say, " that it might be fulfilled which was spoken by the prophets." Their real meaning would be better conveyed to us by such words as " so that it was fulfilled." The Crucifixion they always treated as a monstrous crime and a supreme sin, and they never wrestled with the problem how it could be that if it was foreknown and in some sense intended by God. It is quite certain that they did not think of God as the author of sin.

We shall go wrong, in our vain attempt to solve the age-long problem of human freedom and Divine foreknowledge, if we try to find the " necessity " for Christ's death in a " plan of salvation " to be worked out mechanically.

" Who fathoms the eternal thought ?
    Who talks of scheme or plan ?
  The Lord is God ; He needeth not
    The poor device of man." [1]

There was an " objective necessity " for the
death of Christ, but it is vain to look for it in the
mind of God, which we have no power adequately
to conceive.   We find it rather in the circumstances
of the case.[2]   Given his message, his methods, as
against the stubborn prejudices of his contem-
poraries, no other issue was possible.   But they
need not have been, and ought not to have been,
so blind and hard.   Their blind fury was certainly not a part of the Divine purpose for the
world.

The mind of man has tried in vain to reconcile
human freedom with absolute Divine foreknowledge.   If we have to abandon either, the latter
will have to go.   We do not really understand
the nature of Divine omniscience, any more than
of Divine omnipotence, for we have had no
experience of either.   In some sense we are bound
to recognise that human freedom sets limits to
the omnipotence of God, when this is conceived
in terms of power or force ; for He has produced
intelligent persons who have the ability to act
contrary to the law of their being, and so to
frustrate, for a time at least, His purposes for

[1] Whittier, *The Eternal Goodness*.   [2] See. further, p. 129.

them and for the world. We must conceive omnipotence rather in terms of Love, which, without violating freedom, is able, with infinite patience, to overcome even the obstacle of sin. Perhaps human freedom also limits Divine omniscience, if we conceive this in terms of the power to foresee all that will ever happen. If there is real freedom, there must be also contingency; and what free beings can or will do is not determined in any scheme of absolute Divine predestination.

God is not the author of sin. We must beware of any theory of the Atonement which makes the whole tragedy of the Crucifixion a puppet-show; which represents our Lord's weeping over Jerusalem as a piece of play-acting; or which leads to the conclusion that, if its leaders "had known the things that belonged to their peace," neither they nor any of us could have been saved.

CHAPTER V

EARLY AND MEDIEVAL THEORIES

ABSENCE OF EARLY THOUGHT ON THE ATONEMENT

THE Doctrine of Atonement is not to be identified with the "Substitution" theory, which is only one of its forms. The study of the Bible on which we have been engaged shows that there are other ways of explaining the relation of Christ's death to human salvation than the doctrine that he bore in our stead the punishment which was due to us. This chapter will be devoted to a slight sketch of some of the thoughts that held the minds of Christians before the theory of Substitution was elaborated.

In the first two centuries of Christianity there was little thought or speculation about the Atonement. Most Christians were content with the simple belief that "Christ died for our sins, according to the Scriptures" (1 Cor. xv. 3), and felt no need of attempting to explain the matter. Here and there, however, we find pregnant and valuable thoughts thrown out, which show how deeply the sacrifice of Christ was felt. Clement of Rome, writing to the Corinthians about A.D. 95, says :

> " Let us fix our eyes on the blood of Christ, and understand how precious it was unto his Father, because being shed for our salvation *it won for the whole world the grace of repentance*."

The whole efficacy of the death of Christ is here regarded as directed to men, not to God ; it is the chief means of awakening in them the sense of what sin costs the eternal heart of love. Here Clement shows that he had the root of the matter in him.

In the *Epistle to Diognetus*, a defence of the Christian faith addressed, by an unknown apologist, perhaps to the Diognetus who was tutor to the Emperor Marcus Aurelius, about A.D. 150, we have some tender and beautiful thoughts on this subject.[1] After saying that the Jews who practise sacrifice as if it were acceptable to God " are in no way different from those who show the same respect to deaf images," the writer goes on to speak of God sending His Son to men.

> " Was he sent, think you, as any man might suppose, to inspire fear and terror ? Not so. But in gentleness has He sent him, as a king might send his son who is a king. He sent him, as sending God ; He sent him as

[1] The quotations that follow are from the translation in Lightfoot, *Apostolic Fathers*, pp. 505-509.

a man unto men ; He sent him as Saviour, using per-
suasion, not force, for force is no attribute of God. He
sent him as summoning, not as persecuting ; He sent
him as loving, not as judging."

" He hated us not, neither rejected us, nor bore us
malice, but was long-suffering and patient, and in pity
for us took upon Himself our sins, and Himself parted
with His own Son as a ransom for us, the holy for the
lawless, the guileless for the evil, the just for the unjust,
the incorruptible for the corruptible, the immortal for
the mortal. For what else but his righteousness could
have covered our sins ? In whom was it possible for us
lawless and ungodly men to have been justified, save
only in the Son of God ? O the sweet exchange, that
the iniquity of many should be concealed in the one
Righteous Man."

This is the language of religion rather than of
theology, of deeply felt experience and not of
theory.[1]

GREEK THOUGHTS ON ATONEMENT

The early Greek Christians differed much in
their ways of thinking from the Romans, whose
ideas have largely moulded our Western theology.
Broadly, the Greeks sought after Illumination,
the Romans held by Authority. The Greeks

[1] In the *Expository Times* for April 1921, Dr. Adolf Deiss-
mann, of Berlin, gives a long list of early Christian " en-
comia " or appreciations of the power of the Cross, which
show how deeply it moved the minds of simple-minded
Christians in the pre-dogmatic period. They are, he says,
" extraordinarily valuable evidences of the practical religion
of ancient Christianity, that remained indestructible beneath
the surface of the theological religion of the thinkers "

were inclined to think in terms of " substance,"
the Romans in terms of " law." The words
" Light " and " Life " will serve to indicate the
basis of Greek thought : what was desired was
to see truth, and to have a sure hold on immortality. The fear of death was strong among the
Greeks, even after they became Christian ; and
Christ was he who had " brought life and incorruption to light through the Gospel " (2 Tim.
i. 10).

The statement that the Greeks were inclined to
think in terms of " substance " means something
of this kind. Each great class of objects was
regarded as having its " nature " or " substance "
—a kind of subtle essence which made it what
it was. God had His nature, which was pure,
eternal and immortal. Man also had his nature,
which was just the opposite—corrupt, perishable,
transitory. The problem of the Creeds was to
explain how these two " natures " were com-
bined in Jesus Christ. This was the theme on
which the best intellects among the Greek Christians spent their energies, but it does not concern
us now.[1] The problem of salvation, which does
concern us, was, How can man's nature be changed
into God's nature ? This was not for the Greeks
a question of personal relations ; they did not

---

[1] I have dealt with this subject in summary fashion in my
book *Christ in Christian Thought.*

think of personality as we do, and had indeed
no word for " person " in our sense of the term.
Nor was it in the first instance an *ethical* question,
though of course the purity of the Divine nature
involved ethical considerations. The answer to
the question how man's nature could be changed
into the Divine was that to effect this change
God became man in Christ—in order that we, as
the writer of 2 Peter says, " might become partakers of the Divine nature " (2 Pet. i. 4). Hence
the Incarnation, not the Crucifixion, is the centre
of Greek thought about salvation. " God," says
Irenæus, " became what we are, that He might
make us what He is." The word " deification,"
even, is freely used. It was to make us Divine
that Christ became man : the Incarnation, per-
petuated in the Sacrament, held the central
place.

The most careful statement of this doctrine is
by Athanasius, in his work on the Incarnation,
written in the fourth century.[1] Only, he says,
by God becoming man could He bestow on man
immortal life. The forgiveness of sins is necessary, but it is not enough, because it does not
get rid of man's essential corruption. God in
Christ must share our nature to turn it into His.
But Athanasius recognises that salvation is due

[1] For a full exposition of the thoughts of Athanasius, see
Moberly, *Atonement and Personality*, pp. 348–365.

not only to what Christ *was*, but to what he *did*
and what he endured. Biblical language is used
about his paying our debt, but it is not developed
into a theory.

Moberly says truly that " the intellect of the
Church was not seriously at work upon the subject " (of the Atonement).[1] The best evidence of
this is that the great Creeds, which were worked
out in the fourth and fifth centuries, have hardly
a word to say about it.[2] The ideas of the early
Greek theologians regarding Atonement were entirely unsystematic. Sometimes they speak of
the death of Christ as an example to us, sometimes in sacrificial terms as an offering to God.
Their thoughts on the forgiveness of sins were
complicated by the fact that they connected it
with Baptism more than with the death of Christ.
It was mainly, they thought, through the Sacraments, as carrying on the Incarnation, that the
new Divine nature was effected in us ; and their
expressions often tend to represent the change
as mysterious, not to say magical.

---

[1] *Atonement and Personality*, p. 366.
[2] The *Apostles' Creed* (which did not reach its final form
till the eighth century) says that Jesus " suffered under Pontius
Pilate, was crucified, dead and buried." The *Nicene Creed*
(mainly A.D. 325) has the one word " suffered." The *Chalcedonian Creed* (A.D. 451) has nothing at all on the matter. The
Athanasian Creed (fifth century ; it has nothing to do with
Athanasius) says, " who suffered for our salvation." That is
all that appears in the Creeds.

THE RANSOM THEORY

The first real theory of the Atonement was suggested by the words of Jesus (Mark x. 45) about giving his life " as a ransom for many "— words which are echoed in other parts of the New Testament, as in 1 Pet. i. 18 (" redeemed "), and 1 Tim. ii. 6 (" who gave himself a ransom for all "). The word found its echo in the experiences of the times. David Smith has shown, in his book on the Atonement, how familiar people were in those days with having to pay money to brigands or pirates for the release of captives. Brigandage and rebellion were common, at any rate on the frontiers of the Empire, and Roman citizens were often captured and held to ransom. " The thought of captivity was a haunting terror in that age." [1] And so, by analogy, sin was naturally pictured as bondage, Christ as the Redeemer who releases the captives, and his life as the price paid.

As poetry it is suggestive and true, but it was turned into dull prose. The unnecessary question was asked, " To whom was the price paid ? " *Irenæus,* a Greek from Asia Minor who was appointed Bishop of Lyons in Gaul in A.D. 178, and came to some extent under the influence of Roman legal ideas, seems to have been the first

[1] D. Smith, *The Atonement in the Light of History*, pp. 61–65.

to suggest the answer that the price was paid to the Devil. The Devil, he says, had gained possession and acquired a right over us ; and this right had to be recognised by God, who acts justly and not by force. This idea, however, is only thrown out incidentally by Irenæus, whose main thought was, as has been said, that of the " deification " of man.

The Ransom theory was developed by *Origen*, the great Alexandrian teacher, about A.D. 200. In his commentary on Romans he says :

" If therefore we were bought with a price, as Paul also agrees, without doubt we were bought from someone whose slaves we were, who also demanded what price he would, to let go from his power those whom he held. Now it was the Devil who held us, to whom we had been sold by our sins. He demanded therefore as our price the blood of Christ."

Elsewhere he writes :

" But to whom did he give his soul as a ransom for many ? Certainly not to God, why not then to the Devil ? For he had possession of us until there should be given him the ransom for us, the soul of Jesus : though he was deceived by thinking that he could have dominion over it, and did not see that he could not bear the torture caused by holding it." [1]

There are indications that Origen himself regarded this theory as an explanation suited for immature minds, rather than as one that fully

[1] Quotations from Franks, *The Work of Christ*, vol. i. pp. 56, 57.

satisfied himself. He thought there was a higher stage of Christian experience, in which ideas about redemption would be transcended. " Happy are they who no longer need the Son of God as physician or shepherd or redemption, but as wisdom and word and righteousness." [1]

We note how he suggests that the Devil was deceived by God. This idea can be traced back in early Christian writings, and it probably arose from Paul's words in 1 Cor. ii. 8 about " God's wisdom, which none of the rulers of this world knoweth ; for had they known it they would not have crucified the Lord of glory." By " the rulers of this world " Paul probably meant not the High Priest and Pilate, but the angelic or demonic powers to which he alludes in Eph. vi. 12 as " the world-rulers of this darkness." The idea of a trick practised on Satan, by which he thought he was getting a price, but found not only that he could not keep it but that it overthrew his power, appears elsewhere in Origen's writings, and frequently in those of other theologians. Some of them suggested that God purposely veiled His Divinity in Christ under the form of humanity, as a hook is covered by the bait ; and Satan, swallowing the bait, found himself caught by the hook. God used guile, in order that Satan might be rewarded after his deserts,

[1] Mozley, *The Atonement*, p. 104.

and that the trick might end in human salvation—
by which, one of these writers hints, even Satan
himself would receive benefit in the end. Another
metaphor, which seems to have originated with
Augustine, is that the Cross was a mouse-trap
baited with the blood of Christ.

We have seen that Greek thought centred on
the Incarnation, as at once the revelation of God
and the overcoming in humanity of corruption
and death by the infusing of a pure immortal
life. But the idea of a ransom paid to Satan
was closely connected with this, because corruption and death were attributed to, and almost
personified in, an evil power, the Devil, who was
regarded as intensely real. (Compare Heb. ii. 14,
" and might bring to nought him that had the
power of death, that is, the devil.") Grotesque
and childish as the Ransom theory is, in its
developed form, it does at least preserve the
thoughts of the bondage of sin, and of the love
and self-sacrifice of God in giving His Son to
deliver us from it. It does not represent God
as visiting His wrath on His well-beloved Son ;
and it is quite consistent with the sunny thoughts
of God which we find in Greek Christians like
Clement of Alexandria. The belief in the victory
of Christ over the demonic powers, of which
Satan was regarded as the chief, was an intense
relief to minds that had been haunted all their

lives with fears of evil spirits ; [1] and it is still of
value among peoples where such fears prevail.
But for us its meaning is largely gone. The
Ransom theory goes to pieces on the idea of a
transaction between God and the Devil, which is
a bit of speculative mythology without any basis
in experience ; and also on that of a *trick* practised
on Satan by the Father, which is unworthy of
the character of God as revealed by Christ. Yet
it dominated the minds of Christians for nearly
a thousand years.

ROMAN THOUGHT

The Roman mind, as contrasted with the Greek,
was practical, unmystical and unphilosophical. It
had little confidence in either Insight or Reason,
and its beliefs rested mainly on Authority. What
was handed down as true, by those who were
supposed to know, must be accepted. The Latins
thought mainly in terms of Law. They had a
definite idea of *persons*, as having a certain
" status " determined by legal arrangements. They
did not think of God in the Greek manner as
immanent Spirit and absolute Reality, incorruptible and immortal, but in rather hard personal
terms, as a magnified Governor or Judge. While
the idea of Christ's death as a ransom paid to

---

[1] It should be noted that the Sacraments were also regarded
as having a demon-expelling power.

Satan still held the field, they tended to regard it more and more as a legal transaction, the payment of a debt.

The greatest names are Tertullian (A.D. 150–225), Ambrose (died 395), and Augustine of Hippo (354–430). With *Tertullian* began belief in " original sin," that is, inherited guilt and corruption ; and he also popularized lurid ideas of a material hell. The term " satisfaction " begins to be freely used concerning the work of Christ. This is at first distinguished from punishment. If a person could not pay a debt, he might do something else that would be taken as an equivalent. Hence (with Tertullian) begins the disastrous idea of *works of merit*—such as fasting, prayer, self-abasement—whereby men might satisfy God and win desert in His sight. But, since such works were often regarded as " penance " or self-chastisement, the ideas of satisfaction and punishment were not always kept clearly distinct. Christ by his voluntary death was looked upon as discharging our debt ; his death was the supreme act of merit in the sight of God, and so it made satisfaction to Him.

Ambrose says : " Christ underwent death that the sentence (of death) might be fulfilled, and that satisfaction might be made to the judgment. Nothing was therefore done in opposition to the sentence of God, since the condition of the Divine sentence was fulfilled." [1] Elsewhere he says: "The person rather than the sentence was changed." [2] Here is the germ of later theories of Penal Substitution ; the idea of sacrifice is being interpreted as satisfaction, and even as punishment.

Augustine, the great African bishop, was a man of genius, whose intense Christian experience and extraordinary powers of thought profoundly influenced Christianity till long after the Reformation. But his mind was so varied and comprehensive that it is impossible even to outline his views, which changed much, even after his conversion. Whatever he touched he dealt with in such an intense way that his thoughts became a mine from which later theologians dug, even if they belonged to quite different schools of thought. To him in the main we owe the belief in total human depravity, irresistible Divine grace, the predestination of the " elect " for salvation, and so forth. But we can hardly discover in his writings any logically complete or consistent theory of the work of Christ.

He assumes as fundamental the Ransom theory, but more and more it is regarded as necessary to satisfy Divine *justice,* which must " give even the Devil his due." But this Justice becomes

[1] Franks, *The Work of Christ,* vol. i., p. 111.
[2] Rashdall, *Idea of Atonement,* p. 328.

divorced from the thought of Fatherhood. The human race lies under a just curse of damnation, and all are children of wrath. Christ "placates this wrath" (these are Augustine's words) "by the offering of a unique sacrifice, of which all the sacrifices of the law and the prophets were shadows." [1] At the same time Augustine in other passages writes warmly and powerfully of the love of God, as working love in us through the sacrifice of His Son.

Roman theology is marked by an overpowering sense of sin and of the need of Atonement. But this is associated with dark and terrible thoughts of God, from which the idea of Fatherhood in any real sense has almost disappeared. There is little in it of the sunshine that shone in the soul of Clement of Alexandria. Its redeeming feature, however, is its hold on the humanity of Christ, and of his real suffering for us. With the Greeks, in spite of the Chalcedonian definition (A.D. 451) of the true humanity of Christ (which was mainly due to the great Latin, Pope Leo) the thought of the humanity was largely obscured, except among the Nestorian Christians. Some of them spoke freely of Christ's *impersonal* humanity. If they thought of him as Man, this was rather in an abstract and general sense as representing all humanity; he was for them hardly *a* man, with

[1] Franks, *The Work of Christ*, vol. i., p. 122.

a definite personal character and experience. But
the Roman insistence on his real suffering, good
as it was, tended to contrast his love with the
severity of God (miscalled His " justice "), and
to draw men's love to the Son and not to the
Father.

Another merit of the Roman theology is its
placing of the seat of sin *in the will* (and the con-
sequent recognition of the ethical character of
Divine Grace), and not in some essential corruption of " nature," which could be transmuted by
semi-magical means. But the *total* incapacity of
the human will for good, as laid down by Augustine
and others, was a violent over-statement, which
has no foundation in the teaching of Jesus.

The Doctrine of Satisfaction

We pass on now to the Middle Ages, from
about A.D. 1000 to 1500. Medieval thoughts
about the Atonement were largely moulded on
the lines of ecclesiastical *penance*, and their form
is mainly due to Tertullian and Augustine.
Penance, as we have seen, was not regarded in
the first instance as punishment, but rather as
a legal equivalent or compensation for wrong
done to God. We may compare it to the
" damages " imposed by a civil court as contrasted with the sentence of punishment declared
by a criminal court. The idea was in harmony

with the practice of " wergild " or compensation, the honour-price set on the life of every free man according to his status in society.

David Smith, in his book on the Atonement, connects the idea of Satisfaction with the medieval notions of *chivalry*. The stain on a man's " honour " set by an insult could only be wiped out by " satisfaction," as in the duel. This may have been a contributing factor ; what is certain is the connection of the idea of Satisfaction with the practice of Penance, as something acceptable to God, to " atone " for the wrong done to Him.

The method of medieval theology is mainly the use of logic, to show the reasonableness of the doctrines taught by the Church. These doctrines were taken for granted, on the threefold authority of Scripture, the Creeds, and the expositions of the Fathers, especially Augustine. Within these limits the attempt was made to systematise all Christian doctrine by the use of Reason. Dr. Franks speaks of " the complete confidence in logic, and the surprising dexterity in its use," [1] which these ages revealed. There was undoubtedly a powerful intellectual revival during the eleventh century.

The greatest figure of the time is that of *Anselm* (1033-1109), who was Archbishop of Canterbury under William Rufus and Henry I.

[1] *The Work of Christ*, vol. i., p. 157.

He was a man of strong and saintly character, and had immense influence in Europe. It was he who built up the power of the Church as against the State in England. His greatest book is called *Cur Deus Homo ?* (best translated, perhaps, " Why a God Man ? ")—written to explain the necessity for the Incarnation. The Incarnation, Anselm says, was necessary to make possible the Atonement ; for only one who was absolutely God as well as man could offer to God the satisfaction required because of man's sin.

Sin, Anselm argues, is failure to give to God the honour that is His due. God cannot simply pass this by, for to do so would be to admit something *out of order* in His kingdom. Either the honour taken away must be replaced, or man must be punished. (Anselm draws a sharp distinction between the two.) No penance that a man can offer is enough, because it is already due to God. Besides, man is powerless to render it because of sin. Sin is of infinite gravity, because it is against the infinite God ; it can only be atoned for by an infinite satisfaction, and this man, being finite, can never offer. (These quantitative ideas are characteristic of the time.) Hence only a God-man, who is both man and infinite, can make the satisfaction that is required.

But why should not the perfect *life* of Christ have sufficed, without his death ? Because,

Anselm says, this was due to God in any case. His death was not so due; it was something beyond what could be expected; and, being the death of an infinite Being, voluntarily endured, it had infinite value in God's sight. Thus the necessary satisfaction was made, and man was delivered from infinite punishment.

This is the " Satisfaction Theory," and it gave the death-blow to that of the Ransom paid to the Devil. We note that the satisfaction is not paid to the Devil, but to God; also that Christ is not *punished* by God, but saves man by offering a *gift* to Him—the gift of perfect obedience, even to death.

If we compare this with the early Greek view, we notice that they agree in ascribing Salvation to the whole work of Christ, and not exclusively to his death. But (apart from the Ransom theory) the Greek Christians conceived the work of Christ *mystically*, as having a direct (possibly even a magical) effect in man, changing his corrupt and perishable nature into Divine incorruption, bringing him light and immortality. By Anselm it is thought of *rationally*, as a legal transaction quite outside man himself: a gift made to God which alters His attitude towards us, and enables Him to save instead of punishing us. Christ gives up his life to God, and in return God gives us salvation. A change in man *follows*, but is not a necessary part of, the Atonement. This defect is fundamental in all substitutionary theories.

Anselm's doctrine of Satisfaction replaced, as has been said, the Ransom theory, and remained dominant till the Reformation. It is worked out, for the most part, independently of the New Testament, where nothing is said about God's honour or the need of compensation. All these theories mark a cold drop from the glow and elevation of the early experience which inspires the New Testament writings, and some of those in the pre-dogmatic days of Christianity, like the Epistle to Diognetus.

The Moral Influence Theory

A few words should be added here about the doctrine advanced by *Abelard* (1079–1142)—a man of erratic genius and troubled life, who was far in advance of his time, and who suffered much from this and because of his passionate and ill-regulated life. He attempted, but never completed, a thorough system of Christian doctrine on medieval lines. It is in his commentary on Romans that his thoughts on Atonement appear.

He rejects in the first place the Ransom theory—partly because he accepts from Augustine the view that Christ redeemed only *the elect*, and these were never in Satan's power. He also rejects Anselm's idea that Christ by his death made satisfaction to God, on the ground that God could never " be delighted with the death of the innocent." He finds the real secret of Christ's salvation to lie *in the kindling of love in us*, by his perfect self-sacrifice. " Our redemption," he says, " is that supreme love (kindled in us) by the passion of Christ, which not only frees us from slavery to sin, but acquires for us the true liberty of the sons of God ; so that we fulfil all things, not so much from fear, as from love of him who exhibited so great favour towards us." [1] Abelard does not explain how the awakening of love in us is connected with the forgiveness of our sins except by an allusion to Luke vii. 47 (" her sins, which are many are forgiven, for she loved much "), the meaning of which he misunderstands. But he does show with power how the kindling of love in us sets the will free for joyful obedience.

The view which he adumbrates is often called the " Moral Influence Theory," and it is the starting-point of the modern view of the Atonement. It appears to have been quite new in theology. Dr. Franks says that " it does not coincide with any tendency of previous doctrine." Yet everyone who used the New Testament must have found thoughts like those of Abelard abundantly suggested there.

[1] Rashdall, *Idea of Atonement*, p. 358.

He had a small following among some of the Schoolmen, but the Church as a whole was not ready for so revolutionary a doctrine. He was bitterly attacked by Bernard of Clairvaux, who upheld the Ransom theory and charged Abelard with teaching nothing more than Christ's moral example. Through Bernard's influence he was sentenced to perpetual imprisonment for teaching unorthodox doctrine, but was eventually allowed to remain secluded in the abbey of Cluny. Bernard insisted on what is called an " objective " view of Redemption—that is, that the sacrifice of Christ must have had some meaning and value apart from any change it works in us ; and this difference about the nature of Atonement is with us still.

CHAPTER VI

THE DOCTRINE OF SUBSTITUTION

THE theory of Anselm, that Christ made atonement for human sin by satisfying the honour of God which sin had outraged, held the field on the whole until the Reformation. Erasmus, indeed, who died in 1536, and whose mind was full of the newly discovered New Testament in Greek, pleaded for a return to the simplicity of Scripture ; but he virtually put aside the need for Redemption, and for simple people, he thought, all that was necessary was that they should follow the perfect example of Christ.

THE REFORMATION : LUTHER AND CALVIN

With *Martin Luther* (1483–1546) came a complete break with Church authority, which had till then been dominant. All ideas of human merit through penance and self-mortification, and with these the Satisfaction theory, were discarded ; but the need for Redemption, as the centre and heart of Christianity, was firmly held.

Luther was essentially the prophet of the new

order—a man of genius, with an intense religious experience arising out of his rediscovery of the Pauline dictum that " the just shall live by faith." Like Augustine, he was not a logical or consistent thinker ; he felt, indeed, nothing but contempt for human reason. But he had a similar intense realisation of the truths that were clear to him, and an extraordinary power of vivid and concrete expression. His dependence was neither on Church authority nor on reason, but on intuition— in the sense of an insight into the meaning of Scripture, which he interpreted in accordance with his own inner experience. " No man," he said, " sees an iota in the Scripture but he that has the Spirit of God." Anything, even in the Bible, that seemed to contradict his spiritual intuition he felt himself free to reject as uninspired, like the Epistle of James, which he called " a right strawy Epistle," because it did not teach justification by faith. The Creeds he accepted as summarising Scripture, but all other theologising he laid aside. He made a new start, on what he thought to be the revelation contained in the New Testament.

He believed in " original sin " even more thoroughly than did Augustine. The Fall " brought us into open and rebellious disobedience to God, death and all dangers ; so that we lay under His wrath, condemned to perpetual damnation, as we had merited by our guilt." Christ came to earth, and by taking on himself the penalty of death freed us from this awful doom. He " delivered us poor wretched sinners from the jaws of hell, saved us and guaranteed us liberty ; won the favour and grace of the angry Father by placating His wrath, and took us as His own possession." [1]

This salvation becomes ours through " faith "— that is, acceptance of what Christ has done for us. Works of merit, such as penance, have no place in our redemption. All hangs on the forgiveness of sins, and this no works can win. " Where there is the forgiveness of sins, there is both life and salvation." " God reputes us as just and holy for the sake of Christ our Mediator ; and although sin in the flesh is not yet clear taken away and dead, yet God will not impute that to us or remember it." [2] And yet Luther teaches that good works must *follow* the faith that saves, though they will always be imperfect. " Where good works do not follow, there faith is false and not true." This is one of the clearest instances of what Dr. Franks calls Luther's " fundamental irrationalism." Good works are not necessary for salvation, yet they are necessary ; and the contradiction is never cleared.

[1] Quoted (from the Larger Catechism) by Franks, *The Work of Christ*, vol. i., p. 364.

[2] Franks, *op. cit.*, vol. i., p. 373.

Luther's doctrine of Atonement is a development and a hardening of that hinted at by Ambrose and others,[1] that Christ saves us by enduring our punishment and so delivering us from God's wrath. " He could have satisfied for the sins of the world by one least drop of his blood, but now he has satisfied abundantly." [2]   Luther uses the word " satisfied," but not in the same sense as Anselm.   It is not the Divine " honour," but the Divine " justice," that Christ's death satisfies—understanding by " justice " simply the Divine wrath against sin and the necessity of visiting it with death.

John Calvin (1509–1564) was the most able and systematic thinker of Protestantism, and stands at the head of the Reformed Church, as Luther does at the head of the Lutheran.   The main difference between them, apart from the doctrine of the Sacraments, turned on whether Christ died for all men, or for the elect only. Calvin held the latter view,[3] and it is the more logical.   For if, as has been often said, Christ bore the exact punishment that was due to man's sin, then the unsaved have to bear it *over again*, and there is an obvious failure in Divine justice.   God for Calvin, as for Luther, is the Supreme Ruler

[1] See above, pp. 99, 100.
[2] Franks, *The Work of Christ*, p. 378.
[3] His own expressions are not perfectly clear about the limitation, but those of some of his successors are.

of the world, and supremely " just." His justice requires in every case the penal retribution which sin has deserved—this is the cardinal belief of these Reformation theologians.

Human sin, in Calvin's view, is absolute : man is totally depraved, and has lost all freewill to goodness. Only God can save him, and those whom God chooses to save are the elect. This He does through Christ, who suffers the necessary punishment in their place. God graciously provides a substitute, that on him the inevitable wrath may fall.

" The principal point of our reconciliation with God was that man, who had lost himself by his disobedience, should by way of remedy oppose to it obedience, satisfy the justice of God, and pay the penalty of sin. Therefore our Lord came forth very man, adopted the person of Adam and assumed his name, that he might in his stead obey the Father ; that he might present our flesh as the price of satisfaction to the just judgment of God, and in the same flesh pay the penalty which we had incurred. Finally, since as God only he could not suffer, and as man only he could not overcome death, he united the human nature with the Divine, that he might subject the weakness of the one to death as an expiation for sin, and by the power of the other, maintaining a struggle with death, might gain us the victory." [1]

While Calvin speaks of Christ as " restoring us to the Divine favour," he yet recognises that it was out of the Divine favour that Christ was

[1] *Institutes*, xii., § 3. (Franks, *op. cit.*, p. 428.)

given us. Here he is hardly more logical than was Luther. He thinks he removes the apparent contradiction by saying, after Augustine, that " God loves the sinner, but hates his sin." But " sin " is not an entity in itself ; it has no reality except in a sinning person ; and it is the person, not the " sin," that in Calvin's thought has to be punished. And neither Calvin nor anyone else has been able to show that the " justice " which demands penal retribution *for its own sake* is the same thing as love.

The means of God's reconciliation to us (that is, to the elect) is the whole life of Christ, but especially his death. Here the whole curse laid on us was transferred to him, and so guilt is no longer imputed to us. But the punishment Christ endured was not mere physical death ; the price of our redemption was spiritual. That is to say, Christ endured damnation in our stead. He " bore in his soul the tortures of condemned and ruined man." This awful doctrine Calvin thinks he proves from the agony in the Garden and on the Cross. Others so interpreted the words of the Apostles' Creed, " he descended into hell," which are based on a strange and misinterpreted passage (1 Pet. iii. 19), where Christ is said to have " preached unto the spirits in prison."

Like Luther, Calvin rejects antinomianism (the doctrine that for the believer there is no moral law), but at a similar sacrifice of strict logic. " So long as we are without Christ and separated from him, nothing which he suffered and did for the human race is of the least benefit to us. To communicate to us the blessings which he received from the Father, he must become ours and dwell in us." " No man will know him aright without at the same time receiving the sanctification of the Spirit." [1] For this union with Christ and experience of sanctification faith is the means ; but faith is God's gift, and therefore our whole salvation depends on God alone. Everything in the last resort hangs on " the Divine decree "— that is, on God's inscrutable and arbitrary will, which has chosen some for salvation and others for damnation. Some of Calvin's successors did not shrink from the logical conclusion that in the case of the latter God is the author of their sin.

This is the extreme form of the Doctrine of Substitution in its penal form. It is often known as the " Forensic " theory, in which God is the despotic Ruler or Judge, and the destiny of man is conceived, in the terms of the law courts, as acquittal or condemnation. It largely ruled the thoughts of Protestant Europe for two or three hundred years, and spread with the Pilgrim Fathers to the Western World. It contains, as we

[1] Franks, *The Work of Christ*, vol. i., pp. 436, 437.

have seen, two fundamental contradictions that were never resolved :

(1) That, while salvation springs entirely from the love of God the Father to His erring children, He needed to be reconciled to them by sacrifice.[1]

(2) That, while the life of practical righteousness is not in any sense a condition of salvation, yet salvation will not be obtained by any in whom righteousness is not brought forth.

THE SOCINIAN CRITICISM

The Doctrine of Substitution was subjected to very severe criticism in the same century in which it was first popularly taught—by *Laelius Socinus*, who died in 1562, and his nephew, *Faustus Socinus*, who died in 1604. Both were very influential in Poland and Northern Italy, and it is from their criticism that modern Unitarianism has sprung.[2] They denied original sin and absolute predestination, and held that man could do right if he chose. Christ was a perfect man who became immortal and revealed to men the perfect

[1] If Christ, who offers the sacrifice in himself, is thought of as a separate being from God, all our love is drawn to him and not to the Father. If he is regarded as one with the Father, there is a division in the Divine nature which cannot be reconciled either with the New Testament or with reason.

[2] It is significant that many " Presbyterian " churches became Unitarian. The idea that the Son placated the Father's wrath necessarily tended to divide the Son from the Father, since it was impossible to maintain with reason that the Father placated Himself.

life, confirming the truths he taught by his death and resurrection. They rejected the Protestant idea of Divine " justice " : it was not necessary that God should punish sin. The transference of guilt was impossible, and if possible would be unjust. Christ did not *in fact* endure our punishment, which was eternal death ; he conquered death and rose again. The purpose of his coming was to enable men to become holy, the one thing needful, yet the one for which the Protestant dogma found no real and necessary place—for, if Christ has done all, there remains nothing for us to do.

The Socinians held human reason competent to understand and interpret Scripture. They showed that the Protestant doctrine could not be held by reason alone, and they rejected Luther's requirement of " the Spirit," that is, an intuition arising from personal revelation. While their devotion to reason made their exposition of Christianity somewhat hard and cold, their common-sense interpretation of the Bible was of great value, and proved that many of the leading doctrines of Protestant orthodoxy are not really Scriptural.

THE ARMINIANS

Jacob Arminius (or Herrmann), who died in 1609, was converted to disbelief in Calvinism by trying to support it, and reached a position midway between Calvinism amd Socinianism. He agreed with Luther that Christ died for all, and not for the elect only, but he rejected original sin, total depravity, and predestination. The assertion of human freewill is the keynote of Arminian theology. Man is free to choose aright, free to accept or reject the offer of salvation, and he is not so totally corrupt that he cannot use his reason for the interpretation of Scripture. God is not bound by any necessity of His nature to punish sin or to demand satisfaction. Christ did indeed bear sufferings that we had deserved, but there was no strict equivalence between his sufferings and ours, and he was not punished by God. His voluntary self-sacrifice wrought our reconciliation to the Father. Here the strict logic of Calvinism is softened by some true perception of the Divine character as revealed by Jesus Christ.

The greatest of the Arminian theologians was *Hugo Grotius* (1583–1645), the jurist. He wrote an important book, *The Satisfaction of Christ*, in answer to Socinus, to maintain what he thought was the Catholic belief, and he seems to have been unaware that he was departing from the " orthodox " path. His doctrine is sometimes called the " Governmental theory," and it differs in some important respects from that of Luther and Calvin, though it is still cast entirely in the language of the law courts. He represents God as dealing with men not as a *Judge*, who has to administer the law as he finds it, but as the *Moral Governor* of the world, who makes the law Himself, and who has to consider not the interests of the few, but the interests of all. If He forgave sin simply on repentance, this would make the mass of men careless about it. He " willed to use the sufferings and death of Christ as a weighty argument against the immense guilt of us all." Thus He shows at once His hatred of sin and His respect for His own law.

"The Governmental theory agrees with the Moral theory (as set forth by Abelard), in that it conceives the nature of the Atonement as determined by the moral effects which it is designed to promote ; but it differs from the latter in the fact that the motive to which the Atonement appeals is conceived as fear rather than as love. In Christ's death men see what will be their fate if they do not repent, and so are moved to repentance and faith." [1]

It is in some such form as this that the Atonement is still viewed by Christians who, while horrified at the picture of God drawn by Calvin, reject the Abelardian doctrine as purely subjective, and demand some objective necessity for the death of Christ. The chief modern representatives of

[1] *Encyclopædia of Religion and Ethics*, vol. v., p. 646.

the Arminian theology are the Methodists, but it
is also held by many Protestants of different
denominations.

THE QUAKERS

The Quaker movement of the seventeenth
century was a revolt against the dry scholasticism
of Calvin's successors, as the Lutheran was against
that of the Catholic Church.   Both movements
arose directly out of the intense religious experience
of one man, which found its witness in the souls
of others.   All along the Mystics (both Catholic
and Protestant) had taught of a Reconciliation
with God which was not outward or transactional,
but inward and experimental.[1]   The early Quakers
were, without doubt, influenced by their teachings,
though for the most part, it seems, unconsciously.

George Fox (1624–1691) made the discovery of a
great Light from God in his own soul, and inferred
that it shone, at least potentially, in the souls
of all men.   This was a rediscovery of the Imma-
nence of God, which had been prominent in the
early Greek thought of the Logos, but had been
almost totally obscured by Western legal conceptions.   There was, however, no language avail-
able to the first Quakers in which it could be
adequately set forth.

---

[1] See Rufus Jones, *Studies in Mystical Religion*, and *Spiritual
Reformers of the Sixteenth and Seventeenth Centuries*.

The word " Atonement " is rare in their writings. But everywhere they insist on the universality of the grace or love of God, in opposition to the ruling Calvinistic dogma of arbitrary predestination. God had manifested His " grace " by implanting in all men's souls a Divine Light. This Light, though they usually spoke of it as the Light of Christ, they never properly co-ordinated with the revelation brought by the life and death of Jesus, but they held to the latter also. It was not made central in their teaching, but was rather taken for granted. It is fully acknowledged in the manifesto issued by George Fox and others in 1671, and addressed to the Governor of Barbadoes :

" This Jesus is our foundation, who tasted death for every man, shed his blood for all men, and is the pro-pitiation for our sins, and not for ours only, but also for the sins of the whole world. . . . He alone is our Redeemer and our Saviour, who saves us from sin as well as from hell and the wrath to come. . . . He is our Mediator, that makes peace and reconciliation between God offended and us offending, he being the oath of God, the new covenant of light, life, grace, and peace, the author and finisher of our faith." [1]

All this they never thought of denying. But their chief emphasis was laid on the necessity that Salvation should be an experience and a life,

[1] Fox's *Journal* (Bicentenary Edition), vol. ii., pp. 155–158.

not a mere dogma learned and held by the mind. It was not to be won by any belief in a doctrine, however true, but only by experimental knowledge. Christ, as the Mystics said, must be crucified *in us*: "the Cross," George Fox was never tired of insisting, "is the power of God." The essence of Christianity was an inward cleansing; holiness was not something that simply *followed* "justification" but had no necessary connection with it. There could be no pretence or make-believe with God who was the Truth; and what He required of us was real, and not fictitious righteousness.

James Nayler, who (in spite of his temporary fall into extravagance) was one of the most beautiful spirits in the Quaker movement, urges that it is the Light within that reveals to man his sinfulness, brings him to repentance, and *leads up to justification and peace*. For him, justification cannot be separated from actual righteousness.[1]

Isaac Penington, the Mystic, writes (about 1660) in words that all the "Friends" would have accepted:

"The Quakers believe that Christ is the eternal light, life, wisdom, and power of God, which was manifested

[1] *The Power and Glory of the Lord*, quoted by Brayshaw, *The Quakers, Their Story and Message*, p. 48.

in that body of flesh which he took of the virgin ; that he is the king, priest, and prophet [Calvin's words] of his people, and saveth them from their sins by laying down his life for them and imputing his righteousness to them ; yet not without revealing and bringing forth the same righteousness in them which he wrought for them. And by experience they know that there is no being saved by a belief in his death for them without being brought into a true fellowship with him in his death, and without feeling his immortal seed of life raised and living in them." [1]

Robert Barclay, the author of the *Apology* (1675), says the same at greater length. His main contention is that salvation is gained through obedience to the Light in the soul ; but " we do not hereby intend in any way to lessen or derogate from the atonement and sacrifice of Jesus Christ, but on the contrary do magnify and exalt it. . . . We firmly believe that it was necessary that Christ should come, that by his death and sufferings he might offer up himself a sacrifice to God for our sins. . . . We believe that the remission of sins, which any partake of, is only in and by virtue of that most satisfactory sacrifice, and no otherwise. For it is by the obedience of that one that the free gift is come upon all to justification." [2]

On the basis of this last passage (Rom. v. 18) he frequently speaks of the Light of Christ in

[1] Penington's *Works*, vol. i., p. 360.
[2] *Apology for the True Christian Divinity*, Prop. vi., § 15.

the soul as having been "purchased" for us by the death of Christ—which is going beyond what Paul can have meant. He even speaks at times as if there would have been no grace of God if Christ had not died to procure it; contrary to the teaching of the New Testament, he writes of the death of Christ "reconciling God to us." And yet on the same page he says, as the New Testament does, "the coming of Christ and his propitiatory sacrifice were the fruit of God's love to the world." This inner contradiction he never removes, any more than did Luther and Calvin.

On the whole, the Quakers threw little fresh light on the theory; where they were strong was in *experience* and practice. Their most characteristic and valuable contribution was their insistence that Salvation is essentially an inward work, changing us into the image of God—into His *moral* likeness, and not (as with the Greeks) into His metaphysical essence. Their thought of God was far nearer to that of the New Testament than were the prevailing conceptions of their day.

One of Barclay's best passages is in full line with the Pauline mysticism :

"Justification depends on the formation of Christ in us, from which good works as naturally proceed as fruit from a fruitful tree. . . . By this comes that communication of the goods of Christ unto us by which we come to be made partakers of the Divine nature, and are made one with him as the branches with the vine, and have a title and right to what he hath done and suffered for us ; so that his obedience becomes ours, his righteousness ours, his death and suffering ours." [1]

In other words, the root of the matter is that Christ makes himself one with us, that we may make ourselves one with him, and grow up into his moral image. The thought, like that of Paul, is one of identification, not of substitution.

In harmony with this was the expression, common in early Quaker writings, of the " Suffering Seed " —suggested perhaps by Rev. xiii. 8—carrying the thought that the Divine heart of love has always been suffering for men in the souls of His righteous people, and that these sufferings, exemplified for instance in Jeremiah, are part of His redemptive work, fully manifested in Jesus Christ. Fox records in his *Journal* how, when he was a youth and in sore spiritual trouble, he was catechised by the " priest " of his native village, who asked him why Christ on the Cross exclaimed, " My God, my God, why hast Thou forsaken me ? " Fox replied that at that time the sins of all mankind were upon him. " This I spake, being at that time sensible in a measure of Christ's sufferings and what he went through." Fox was learning what Paul meant by " the fellowship of his suffer-

[1] *Apology*, Prop. vii., § 3.

ings," and "being made conformable to his death "; he was experiencing the power of the Cross in his own life ; and he reached the conclusion that without such inward knowledge theories of the Atonement are of no avail.

CHAPTER VII

MODERN THOUGHT ON THE ATONEMENT

SCHLEIERMACHER AND RITSCHL

THE Substitutionary view of the Atonement, generally in its milder and more Arminian form, remained as the prevailing doctrine among English-speaking people during the eighteenth and a considerable part of the nineteenth centuries. Meanwhile a revolution in theological thinking was being wrought in Germany, chiefly by *Schleiermacher* (1768–1834) and *Albert Ritschl* (1822–1889). Discarding the traditional theology, these thinkers took their stand on Christian experience—as, indeed, the Quakers had to a large extent attempted to do before them. Each of them tried, in his own way, to begin with what Christ has done for the inner life of men, and to discover what beliefs concerning him and his redemption this experience leads to. The movement may be compared to that which in the domain of philosophy was initiated by Kant's enquiry into the foundations of knowledge. Both of them were led to give a very high place to the redeeming work of God in Christ, but both concluded that this could not be rightly stated in forensic terms or those of penal satisfaction. Their thought has been widely influential in Germany, and in other Protestant countries also, and has affected the minds of many who are unaware of the original source of the beliefs which they have come to hold. But it is not possible in this little volume to attempt to outline their views.[1]

Objective and Subjective Views

Confining our study, as seems necessary, to English-speaking thinkers and writers, we notice in the first place that few or none have attempted, like the German theologians who have been mentioned, to systematise or unify all Christian doctrine in the light of a central conception. Their thoughts on the Atonement are mostly to be found either in monographs on the subject, or scattered among their religious writings. Secondly, there is a broad cleavage of views between those who still maintain an " objective necessity " for the death of Christ, and those who explain his saving work in a more subjective or

---

[1] A full presentation of them will be found in Franks, *The Work of Christ*, vol. ii. I have given a slight sketch of their methods of thought in *Christ in Christian Thought*, chap. xxii.

Abelardian manner. Most theologians who hold the " objective " view are not satisfied to find the *main* significance of the death of Christ in its effect on men. It must, they think, be regarded as having in the first place a Godward reference, and as affecting in some way the Divine side of God's relation to men—whether by vindicating His law or keeping intact the moral order of the universe. A little preliminary discussion of such questions may help our survey.

It is, in my judgment, right to say that there must have been some " necessity " for the death of Christ other than its effect on us. If he died *needlessly*, simply to show how much he loved us, this would not be really self-sacrifice, but suicide, and would entirely fail of its purpose. If I were to jump off a pier into deep water simply to show my friend what I would do and endure for him, he would not feel greatful; he would think me mad. But suppose my friend were in the water drowning, and I tried to save him, and then the current carried me away and I got drowned myself. There would be an " objective necessity " for my death here, in the shape of the tidal current ; and it would seem that, in the case of Christ, we may find what we need in the circumstances which he had to meet. Perfect obedience in following the path marked out for him under those conditions meant death, and he

9

knew it, yet " for their sakes he consecrated himself." He did not needlessly seek death, but he met it like a hero in the path of duty.

There are grave difficulties in any view of the Atonement which implies that Christ's death altered the mind of God towards us. One is that it seems to involve a certain separation between His righteousness and His love. His love, we are told, has not free course unless the moral order of the world is preserved intact, as it would not be if sin were simply passed over. Those who hold the " subjective " view demur to this, and say there can be no such conflict in God. His righteousness is perfect love, and must therefore ever strive to communicate itself ; and His love is perfect righteousness, which will let us endure whatever chastisement may be needed to bring us to Him. This difference of view is still strongly felt.

Nineteenth-Century Thought : The Objective View

It seemed desirable to offer these preliminary observations to explain what appear to be the roots of the divergence which still exists on this subject. I now proceed to call attention to a few of the leading British and American thinkers who have specially devoted their minds to it. Among those in whose thoughts an " objective " view predominates I may mention Drs. *R. W. Dale* (1829–1895), *James Denney* (who has recently died), and *J. Scott Lidgett* (who is still living).[1] Of these we may take Dr. Dale as typical. His chief contention, in opposition to Horace Bushnell (whose thoughts we shall be considering later), is that punishment must in the nature of things follow crime as its just retribution, or else Law will not be vindicated. The reformation of the offender, and the prevention of wrongdoing by others, do not (in Dr. Dale's view) exhaust the meaning and purpose of punishment. There is an inner law of the universe that in eternal fitness visits with pain and loss the violation of its order. This law is of God, and He must respect it Himself. So, in the person of His Son, He Himself endures pain and loss in man's stead, that the righteous order of the world may be vindicated.[2] Thus Christ, as at once Divine and the Representative of the human race, restores by his death the ideal relation of humanity to God, which sin had destroyed. There is here no suggestion of *equivalence* between his suffering and ours. It is simply

[1] Dr. Dale's chief book is *The Atonement*; Dr. Denney's is *The Death of Christ*; Dr. Scott Lidgett's is *The Spiritual Principle of the Atonement*.

[2] As Dr. Dale (in full agreement with the New Testament) maintains the unity of Christ with God, it is strange to find him also insisting that on the Cross he was really forsaken by the Father.

that God in Christ suffers pain and death that the moral order of the universe may be preserved.

But will Dr. Dale's foundation hold ? Is it really true that retribution in the shape of pain must be attached to wrongdoing, quite apart from its effect on the offender or others ? Suppose that for a certain crime a punishment is suggested which it is known will have no good effect whatever, either on the offender himself or on anyone else. Could anything justify the infliction of such pain ? Would it not be a wanton addition to the misery of a world already suffering enough ? The doctrine of Retribution, in this sense, is being abandoned by many of the clearest and deepest Christian minds to-day. And, if this goes, so does Dr. Dale's whole theory.

THE SUBJECTIVE VIEW

I will now give a very brief indication of the thoughts of the principal nineteenth-century writers (in this country and in America) who have held a more predominantly " subjective " view.

Samuel Taylor Coleridge (1772–1834), the poet, did for English thought something like what Kant did for that of Germany. He held that no religious doctrine is valid that does not satisfy Reason and Conscience. This, he believed, Christ's redemption does. Sin, he held, is essentially *the will* gone wrong ; and, though it is universal in human experience, it is not inherited. The work of Christ was to conquer sin by giving to men a new will, a new motive ; their redemption was their regeneration. Paul's use of Jewish metaphors of sacrificial expiation must be transcended by us as it was by " John," who spoke of a " new birth "—the actual beginning of a new life *in us*.

" It was necessary that God should be manifested in the flesh, that the Eternal Word, by whom the world was and is, should be made flesh, assume our humanity personally, fulfil all righteousness, and so suffer and die for us as in dying to conquer death for as many as should receive him." [1]

Thus Coleridge thought of Christ as delivering us from sin by his inward work in our souls. There is much in his view that is akin to that of Schleiermacher, and also to the root thoughts of Isaac Penington and other Quakers.

Thomas Erskine, of Linlathen (1788–1870), worked out, quite independently of Coleridge, a similar inward view of Atonement. He also considered that Christianity was self-evidencing, and believed that his doctrine would commend itself to all men's " spiritual reason." Christ, he said, was the Head of our race spiritually, as

[1] *Aids to Reflection*, Ed. 1883, p. 287. (Franks, *The Work of Christ*, vol. ii., p. 376.)

Adam was supposed to be physically, and his
real righteousness was to be reproduced in us.
This was the purpose of the Atonement.

> " Christ did not suffer for men as an individual standing
> *out* of them, and doing something in their stead ; but as
> one *in* them, as the Head of that mass of which they were
> all partakers, as the root of that tree of which they were
> all branches." [1]
>
> " In the Epistle to the Hebrews, Christ is said to have
> put away sin by the sacrifice of himself. I believe that
> nothing but this sacrifice of self can in any case put sin
> away, and that Christ as the Head of the race made this
> sacrifice that it might be reproduced in every member
> of his body." [2]

Frederick D. Maurice (1805–1872), the " Christian Socialist," was greatly influenced by Coleridge
and Erskine, especially the latter. He, with them,
rejected all substitutionary theories. " Like
Erskine, Maurice teaches that in Christ men are
already pardoned, reconciled and redeemed, and
need further only a *consciousness* of this—a subjective experience of the objective Divine fact
accomplished for them in Christ." [3]

McLeod Campbell (1800–1872) was also a disciple
of Erskine. His book, *The Nature of the Atonement*, has been described as " the most systematic

---

[1] *The Brazen Serpent*, p. 55.   (Franks, *op. cit.*, vol. ii., p. 385.)
[2] *The Spiritual Order*, p. 250.
[3] Franks, *op. cit.*, vol. ii., p. 391.

and masterly book on the work of Christ produced by a British theologian in the nineteenth century," and it had a great influence on subsequent British theology. He criticises the ordinary Calvinist doctrine (so largely taught in his day in Scotland) as not revealing the love of God, and as giving to men a *legal* and not a filial standing with Him. But he finds his main starting-point in a hint thrown out by that very thorough-going New England Calvinist, Jonathan Edwards, to the effect that " *a perfect repentance*, had it been possible for man, might have availed as an atonement." Edwards never followed this up, but Campbell does. He says that Christ not only dealt with men on behalf of God, revealing to them at once His holiness and His love, but with God on behalf of men, and this mainly by offering the perfect repentance which man could not offer.

" That oneness of mind with the Father, which toward men took the form of a condemnation of sin, would in the Son's dealing with the Father take the form of a perfect confession of our sins. This confession, as to its own nature, must have been *a perfect Amen in humanity to the judgment of God on the sin of man*." [1]

Christ's sufferings, therefore, were not penal, but purifying and cleansing, working real penitence

[1] *The Nature of the Atonement*, p. 135. (Franks, *op. cit.*, vol. ii., p. 396.)

in us. On the Cross he was not really forsaken by the Father ; his cry of desolation is in the opening words of Psalm xxii, which in verse 24 says : " He hath not despised nor abhorred the afflictions of the afflicted, neither hath he hid his face from him ; but when he cried unto him, he heard." The work of Christ reveals not only the love of God, but the capacity for righteousness latent in humanity ; it produces in us the real righteousness which God requires, and therefore gives us eternal life. He delivers us in the first instance *from sin*, and, incidentally to this, from punishment.

R. C. Moberly (1845–1903), in his book *Atonement and Personality*, follows the same line as Campbell ; but he probes the subject more deeply, in the light of modern philosophic and psychological thought. True punishment, he says, is in its aim not retributive but reformatory ; yet it does not prove reformatory unless it is accepted as discipline. Mere retribution, as such, has no atoning effect at all. Real penitence, as Edwards suggested, would atone ; but *perfect* penitence is impossible for one who has sinned, because sin hardens his character. So far as even imperfect penitence is possible for us, it is due to the indwelling Spirit of the Crucified Christ.

Moberly appears to have been among the first

to examine with any adequacy the true nature of the forgiveness of sins. It is not, he says, mere remission of punishment, but it involves a real change in the offender, who must become " forgivable " before it can be completed. This change in man cannot be effected by a Mediator outside himself, but it is effected by Christ as one with the whole race. In him are realised at once perfect holiness and perfect penitence. This becomes ours by the indwelling in us of his Spirit (this is the chief advance Moberly makes on Campbell's thought), which is more than example, more even than moral influence. Atonement can never be understood while Christ is regarded (as most Western theologians have regarded him) as simply one individual among others. He is an inclusive and pervasive Spirit—" he is more, indeed, than *within* us ; he is the ultimate consummation of ourselves." It is in the Church and its Sacraments that this mysterious union is realised among men.

" We are hundreds of miles from the thought of vicarious punishment. Even if, in a sense, we may consent to speak of vicarious penitence, yet it is not exactly vicarious. He indeed consummated penitence in himself before the eyes and before the hearts of men who were not penitent themselves. But he did so, not in the sense that they were not to repent, or that his penitence was a substitute for theirs. He did so, not as a substitute, not even as a delegated representative, but as that inclusive total of true humanity, of which they were potentially, and were to learn to become [actually], a part." [1]

It will be seen that Moberly's thought of Christ as the "inclusive total of true humanity" marks a return from the rather hard personal categories of the Western theology to the more mystical Greek conception; and it incurs the danger we have already noticed [2] of losing hold on the individual personality of Jesus, and merging him in an abstract or "impersonal humanity." Also, it may well be doubted whether the idea of "vicarious penitence" which he got from Campbell can possibly be held securely; whether anyone can in the true sense be penitent for any sins except his own. The saints and prophets of humanity (such as Jeremiah) have, it is true, been baptized into a profound and often overwhelming sense of the sinfulness of their people, in which they felt themselves so mixed up that at times they seemed almost to lose the consciousness of separate individuality; and such experiences help us to understand something of the victorious conflict which was being waged by our Lord with the powers of evil in Gethsemane and on the Cross. The reality of that great struggle is powerfully impressed by these writers; it is mainly

---

[1] *Atonement and Personality*, p. 283.
[2] See above, p. 101.

the terms they use that seem open to question. What Moberly brings out with special force is Christ's absolute *self-identification* with us, even in our sin and in the alienation from God which it necessarily caused. The agony in the Garden and the cry on the Cross surely mean that by his perfect sympathy, love, and insight he realised in his own consciousness what only the purest hearted can know in its depth of utter anguish— *what sin means* in its alienation of the soul from God.

The dying words of another saint of God, John Woolman, the Quaker pioneer of the great struggle against slavery in America (who died in England in 1772), may be quoted here, as throwing further light on this experience, which brings us, indeed, very near to the heart of our subject:

"O Lord my God! the amazing horrors of darkness were gathered around me and covered me all over, and I saw no way to go forth. I felt the depth and extent of the misery of my fellow-creatures, separated from the Divine harmony, and it was heavier than I could bear, and I was crushed down under it. I lifted my hand, I stretched out my arm, but there was none to help me; I looked round about and was amazed. In the depth of misery, O Lord! I remembered that thou art omnipotent; that I had called thee Father; and I felt that I loved thee, and I was made quiet in thy will, and I waited for deliverance from thee." [1]

[1] *John Woolman, his Life and our Times*, by W. Teignmouth Shore, pp. 265, 266.

Horace Bushnell (1802–1876), an American Congregationalist preacher, wrote an important book on *Vicarious Sacrifice,* which contains perhaps the best modern presentation of the Abelardian view of the Atonement. He says that before Christ came men had the *idea* of God, but it possessed little moral power : it was apt to become cold and thin. It is in Christ that God's moral power operates for men—in all that he was, did, felt, and suffered. What he especially reveals to us is that there is a *human side* in God : he awakens our sense of the personal relation to God which sin has outraged, and at the same time draws out our confidence in Him. He proves by his death that *God suffers* for human sin. Bushnell appears to be almost the first to express clearly this great truth, which has been denied by the majority of theologians in all ages. They have taken it as an axiom that " God cannot suffer," and so, in spite of their theologising, have too often missed the heart of the Atonement. Vicarious suffering and sacrifice is deeply embedded in human experience ; it is a necessary part of human love at its highest and best ; and what is true of human love must also be true of the Divine.

There is, Bushnell urges, no opposition or conflict in the Divine nature between justice and mercy. Justice works through natural law, and mercy does not get rid of the consequences of wrongdoing. But, *by changing us*, it transforms into discipline that which would otherwise be mere punishment. The sacrificial symbols in the Bible Bushnell regards as ways of adumbrating the truth of Divine self-sacrifice. By the use of such terms as " propitiation " men show that they are aware of a wrong relation between themselves and God, and they speak of the righting of this relation as if it meant a change in Him, when the actual change is in themselves. It is much as when we speak of " the sun rising " when what we mean is that the earth turns into the sunlight ; or when a man, pushing off a boat from the shore, seems to himself to be pushing away the land.[1]

Here Bushnell has, in my judgment, found a valuable clue to the use of sacrificial terms, and to the hold they have had, and still have, over many minds. True forgiveness, the restoration of right relations between those who have become estranged from one another, is a difficult and costly thing. In the case of sin against God the obstacle and difficulty that has to be overcome is not on God's side, but on ours ; the language of sacrifice is in part an adaptation to the wrong ideas of God engendered in men's minds by their experience of alienation from Him. As such it may have had, and may still have, an important place in assuring people who wrongly thought of God as

[1] The doctrine of " Relativity " has its place even in theology.

hostile to them that He is not really so.   But, if it is taken too literally, it tends to foster the belief that these ideas represent the truth, and that God needs in some way to be propitiated. The Old Testament guards itself, on the whole, against this (which is the heathen) view, as we have seen.   The Apostles did not press the idea of expiation in such a way as to obscure God's Fatherhood ; and we too must beware of doing so. Our thanks are due to Bushnell for helping to clear a real difficulty out of the way.

CHAPTER VIII

TOWARDS A TRUE DOCTRINE

FACTS THAT MUST BE FACED

THE older theories of Atonement, which many of us find it impossible to hold, owe their strength and persistence largely to the fact that they have faced certain realities which any true doctrine must face. Such are :

(1) Sin is a terrible reality and a hideous and loathsome thing ; and it has fearful consequences, both to the sinner and to others, which need to be brought home to the minds of men. If anyone thinks this statement too strong, let him think of the late war and of its legacy to the world.

(2) The Love of God is no easy-going good-nature, which simply shuts its eyes to evil and leads us to fancy it does not matter much. Forgiveness is not an easy and superficial thing like wiping off bad marks from a slate ; it involves the restoration of right personal relations, and this is difficult and costly, even to God Himself.

(3) Salvation is not to be won by any facile

path of righteousness, as suggested (for example) by Erasmus and Socinus. It requires that we shall be brought down into depths of humiliation and true penitence, where we find our self-righteousness utterly unavailing and of no account.

An ethical and spiritual doctrine of Atonement will only meet the case if it recognises these truths, and faces the yawning chasm there is between our ideal and our actual. The modern view, the progress of which was indicated in the last chapter, does (in measure at least) recognise this chasm. It teaches, as the New Testament also teaches, that the original movement to bridge the gulf comes from the side of God. It is He who reaches across it, taking upon Himself, in the person of Christ, the sacrifice and cost, to show us that the only real obstacle to forgiveness is in ourselves.[1] What man tried to do, with his sacrifices, God Himself has done. He leaves, so to say, the realm of the absolute and the infinite, where it is so hard for us finite beings to reach Him, enters that of the finite and conditioned, becomes a sharer in the temporal and historical order in which we live. In the person of Jesus He lives our life, meets on their own ground the powers of evil, suffers, dies, and conquers.

[1] See Rufus Jones, *The Double Search* (Prayer and Atonement), p. 64.

Is any Doctrine Needed?

But do we still need a " doctrine " of Atonement at all ? Is not the *fact* enough that Christ has saved and does save from sin those who come into a vital relation with himself ? Certainly it is much more important to be redeemed from sin by Christ and to become sharers of his life of love than it is to be able to explain the process. Happily, many know the fact who are quite unable to explain it, and many too whose explanations we may be unable to make our own.

But most of us need an explanation, just because (strange as it may appear) we are fundamentally rational beings. And, in the Divine ordering of the world, Christianity has to be *taught* in words as well as lived. It is right, therefore, that, especially if we are to be in any way teachers of Christianity, we should seek for a doctrine that will satisfy our minds. Some knowledge of the paths along which men have travelled to find an explanation will be of real service to us. We cannot do our best work as Christians in the world unless we try to understand, in order that we may reach the understanding as well as the souls of others. Preaching (if we have to preach) should rarely be argumentative, but it should have a strong foundation in thought ; underlying it there should be a substantial structure of sound brain-work.

Some would say that the Bible is enough. But it is not—just because it needs interpretation. We all tend to interpret it in the light of what we have been taught, and to fancy that our interpretation is the truth. *All* the doctrines we have been studying have some foundation in the Bible—even that of Anselm, in so far as he thought of sin as a debt. The Bible contains no single thought-out doctrine of Atonement, but rather many *suggestions* for a doctrine—it has the material, but not the structure. When we want a suit of clothes we do not go to the spinning mill, still less to the Australian sheep-farm, but to the tailor.

Conditions of a True Doctrine

(1) A sound and satisfactory doctrine of Atonement must start from, and proceed in, the revelation of the character of God which we have in Christ. His consciousness of God as Father was absolutely fundamental in his life; and it was through his perfect experience of Sonship that he revealed the Father to men. His dealing with penitents, as in Luke vii, is a true picture of God's dealing with them. He never suggested satisfaction or expiation; to the woman who had proved her real penitence he said, " Thy faith hath saved thee, go in peace." The experience

and the expressions of his first followers must be interpreted in the light of his own teaching and practice, and not *vice versa*. Their use of sacrificial language was natural under their circumstances, and it brought home to men's minds some realisation of the cost of forgiveness and restoration. But, as has been said, it must not be so used, and they did not so use it, as to obscure the Fatherhood of God. Jesus taught that our experience of human fatherhood is a real clue to an understanding of the Divine. The holier any human father is, the more instant and abundant his forgiveness is, because of his sympathy and his yearning love. God, said Jesus, is like the Shepherd who goes out to seek the lost sheep in the wilderness, and will not rest until he finds it.

(2) A true doctrine must be in harmony with the scientific spirit. That is to say, (a) it must recognise that God works in the world through the operations of natural law ; that every act and event has its natural and inevitable consequences. The forgiveness of sin does not get rid of the consequences sin entails, except by changing the sinner himself ; the consequences of his past sin he has to accept, but forgiveness changes them from punishment into discipline and means of blessing. So far as we can see, this operation of cause and effect covers *all* the Divine punish-

ments of sin.   There is, we may believe, no heavenly
law court in which penalties are dealt out at the
will of a Judge. All this supernatural apparatus
we may regard as imagery. What we know is
that we bring our destiny on ourselves : " as a
man sows, so he also reaps."   Hell is a reality :
it is alienation from God and goodness, the blind-
ing of our inward eyes, the loss of true values,
the hardening of our hearts against love. " *War*
is hell " ; our sin can damn many besides ourselves.
(*b*) But, equally, a scientific view of human life
must recognise, as a fact of experience, the possibility of the moral restoration which Christ's
Gospel offers. This moral reconstruction of life
is found in fact to be chiefly, though not exclusively, the result of a conscious reconciliation to
God through Christ. Other real " conversions "
do occur, and doubtless have often occurred, in
human history. In such cases we must believe
that the Spirit of Christ is at work in men's souls,
but below the threshold of their conscious experience.

(3) It must rest on a sound psychology : that
is, it must be true to the real facts of the religious
life. We must know something of what men and
women do actually experience in regard to the
sense of sin, repentance, forgiveness, conversion.
We must know this by some measure of personal
experience, and not only by observation or reading ;

for without personal experience we shall fail to interpret aright the things we observe or read about. The experiences of different people vary greatly—as we may see by comparing John Bunyan's early struggles, as described in *Grace Abounding*, with the widely different account of himself which his contemporary, George Fox, gives us in his *Journal*.[1] One was full of the sense of personal guilt and the terrors of hell ; the other scarcely mentions such things at all. A true doctrine must be broad-based enough to cover many varieties ; it will fail if it is built on one type of religious experience only. Sound teaching on the forgiveness of sins must have its roots in our psychological experience of human forgiveness at its best, for these are in our Lord's teaching constantly drawn close together : " If ye forgive not, your heavenly Father will not forgive you."

(4) It must do justice to the immensely important place which the Gospels give to the circumstances attending the death of Christ, especially to the agony in the garden and on the Cross. These things must not be explained away. Mysterious as they are, they have gone to the heart of humanity, and any doctrine which ignores them is too shallow.

[1] In this connection Professor William James's book, *Varieties of Religious Experience*, is extremely suggestive.

(5) Account must be taken not *alone* of the sufferings and death of Christ, as though these by themselves were the exclusive means of our salvation, but of his whole life and personality—what he was, taught, and did—his inner experience of Sonship with God, and his perfect obedience right up to death (Phil. ii. 8). His death must not be isolated either from his previous life or from the Resurrection which followed it. However we may be inclined to explain what precisely happened, it was through the Resurrection that his disciples were assured that on the Cross he won the victory.

(6) Atonement must be so regarded as to lead to a salvation that is *social*, and not merely individual. The Kingdom of God must be shown to have a vital connection with the Cross. Ritschl's work is here of special importance. Salvation is not getting into a little private heaven of our own ; it was meant to be as wide as humanity itself. Only as it is so recognised can ardent reformers be convinced that Christ has what they are seeking for. If " our hearts are restless till they rest in God," it is also true, as Mr. Clutton-Brock says, that " His heart is restless till we all rest in Him." [1] Real Christianity must always be missionary, international, and inter-racial, breaking down all the barriers

[1] *Studies in Christianity*, p. 133.

that men set up, including those of caste and class.

In this connection, the belief in human Immortality is seen to be a vital part of any doctrine of Redemption ; for, if physical death ends all, the majority of human beings have no chance of experiencing, consciously at any rate, salvation through the death of Christ. The future life is bound up in our assurance of the universal and saving love of God.

ON THE WAY TO A TRUE DOCTRINE

I believe that, thanks to the labours of many devout Christian thinkers, we are on the way to finding a Doctrine of Atonement that will satisfy both our spiritual and our intellectual needs. Doubtless it will not be complete or final, but it should and may be deep enough, clear enough, strong enough to enable us—if only we ourselves have experienced its power—to speak with joy and confident conviction to our own age with its multitudes of seekers after God.[1]

In Christ and his Cross two great movements in human history converge and meet and culminate : the movement of man in search of communion with God, and of God seeking to reveal Himself to men. God, in the person of Jesus,

---

[1] For some of the thoughts that follow I am mainly indebted to Richard Roberts, *Christ and Ourselves*.

offers to man the priceless gift of perfect reconciliation to Himself. Man, also in the person of
Jesus, gives himself wholly to God, offering Him
the gift of perfect surrender and obedience. In
one Divine Man, and most of all in the crowning
act of his life, God and man meet and blend in
perfect unity : they become *at one*.

(*a*) Look at Atonement first as *the gift of God*.
We need a gift that will in some way actually
take away our *sin*, with its inevitable alienation
of our souls from God and His peace. The Cross
is the supreme manifestation that God does take
it away ; that He forgives it by bearing and
enduring it Himself.

In all true forgiveness there is the bearing of
sin ; and this just in proportion as the forgiveness
is deep and real. The wrong that has been done
hurts, and it costs much to restore the relation
of love and fellowship. The nearer we are to
God in holiness, love, and discernment, the more
it hurts ; it is only the thick-skinned and morally
insensitive who do not feel it. We cannot *really*
forgive anyone's sin against us except as we bear
it ourselves. Even if (an imperfect figure) it is
compared to a debt, he who remits a debt takes
the cost on himself.

Human forgiveness, Jesus taught, is, so far as
it goes, a true picture of the Divine. The father
of the prodigal had been bearing the sin of his

scapegrace son all the years he had been away from home. The Cross reveals to us supremely what the sin of mankind, including *our* sin, has always meant to the eternal heart of love : how it has hurt, how that Divine Love has always been bearing it, mourning over it, seeking to overcome it.   One Divine event shows, under the limitations of time and place and a human personality, what sin and its forgiveness have always, since man first sinned, involved in the inner life of God.

The age-long search of the Divine Shepherd for His wandering sheep, the blood-tracks that mark His footsteps over stones and thorns, the great gift of redeeming grace and reconciliation which He carries for the wanderer, are here expressed. The barrier which blocks the sinner's entrance into the Divine fellowship, which he perhaps imagines to be in God, but which is really in himself, is overthrown.   A " new and living way " is opened up, right into the depths of the Father's heart of love.   " The free gift of God is eternal life, through Jesus Christ our Lord."

(*b*) Then think of Atonement as *man's offering of himself to God*. As Clement of Rome wrote, in days when the fresh intuition of the Cross had not been overlaid with speculation about it, " the blood of Christ, shed for our salvation, won for the whole world the grace of repentance." [1]   Real

[1] See above, p. 89.

repentance is hard, as Moberly has powerfully shown, because sin deadens our spiritual sensitiveness and blinds our eyes to its moral ugliness. The Cross tenders our hearts and opens our eyes, because it reveals the love that sin outrages; and when we really *see* we are brought down in shame and humiliation. The Cross shows us at once the Divine holiness that condemns our sin, and the love that forgives and restores. It is not (as Grotius thought) through fear, aroused by an exhibition of the penal consequences of sin, that we are moved to true repentance, but by love. *Our will must be won*, and this is the essence of Atonement. Force cannot do it; the fear of punishment cannot do it; but love can—and most of all the love that shows us God forgiving sin by taking it on Himself. " The sufferings of Christ represent to us not (as Grotius would have it) an armed demonstration of the Rights of God, but an unarmed, unresisting, albeit resistless, demonstration of the Love of God." [1]

That is the main thought contained in a small book by William E. Wilson, *Atonement and Non-Resistance*, by which he means " Atonement through love to the uttermost." He shows that Love is the essence of Divine Omnipotence : God wins our wills, not by force or threats of punishment, but by the love that bears and forgives.

---

[1] Douglas White, *Forgiveness and Suffering*, p. 112.

When we really see this, we cannot go on wounding One who bears the sin of men as Christ bore the Cross, when he cried, " Father, forgive them, for they know not what they do." " With God all things are possible " (Mark x. 27) : He has the moral dynamic that can turn the great refusal into the great surrender. But it is the moral dynamic of love. That can bring us down into penitence, that can overcome the hardness of our hearts and our divided wills, when nothing else can.

Here we are at the root of things. That was Christ's way of overcoming evil, of winning the world from sin to righteousness ; that is God's way ; that must be our way. Our whole conception of what Christianity is, what it requires from us as a way of life, and how we are to deal with evil in the world, turns on what we see in the Cross.

This thought, however, we must not here attempt to follow out. Let us return to the double gift contained in the Cross—God's gift of Himself to man, and man's gift of himself to God in perfect surrender and obedience. Christ's sacrifice is the manifestation and exhibition of the perfect human obedience that has been and can be rendered, and it avails for us as we unite ourselves to him by faith. God gives Himself to us absolutely, without reserve ; and thereby enables us to give ourselves absolutely to Him, which is our " reasonable service."

From whichever side we regard it, whether as God's gift or as man's gift, the Cross is all of " grace." It is something we could never have devised, something we could never have achieved, something that comes to us from above, renews our wills, and enables us to be and do what God requires of us. When once we *see* the Cross, we start life afresh—the life of self-forgetful service of God and man. The burden of self and of all our unavailing efforts after righteousness falls away, and we are left with nothing of our own— humbled in the dust, yet joyful and confident in the power of Another's love.

" Now I saw in my dream that the highway up which Christian was to go was fenced on either side with a wall, and that wall was called Salvation. Up this way therefore did burdened Christian run, but not without great difficulty, because of the burden on his back. He ran thus till he came at a place somewhat ascending, and upon that place stood a cross, and a little below in the bottom a sepulchre. So I saw in my dream that just as Christian came up with the cross his burden loosed from off his shoulders, and fell from off his back, and began to tumble, and so continued to do till it came to the mouth of the sepulchre, where it fell in, and I saw it no more.

" Then was Christian glad and lightsome, and said with a merry heart, ' He hath given me rest by his sorrow, and life by his death.' Then he stood awhile to look and wonder, for it was very surprising to him that the sight of the cross should thus ease him of his burden. He looked therefore, and looked again, even till the springs that were in his head sent the waters down his cheeks.

Now, as he stood looking and weeping, behold three shining ones came to him, and saluted him with 'Peace be to thee.' Then Christian gave three leaps for joy, and went on singing." [1]

That is how the Cross of Christ makes us new creatures. But it is not only the burden of self that Christ takes from us by his Cross, but the burden, which to some of us is still heavier, of the sin and suffering of the world. He lifts the curtain, and shows the world's greatest sin changed by his obedience into the means of the world's redemption, its most frantic discord changed to harmony. Behind all the agony and chaos and seeming malignity of "this unintelligible world" he shows us the yearning, suffering, redeeming heart of God. That, he assures us, is the inmost core of reality; the deepest nature of things is love. Love has the power, and it will avail, to change the warring wills of men into harmony with the will of God, to bring peace on earth, and the human brotherhood for which we sigh. Thus for the bewildered soul, if only it is faithful and obedient, the world becomes once more a rational order—the preparation for the Kingdom of God.

[1] Bunyan, *The Pilgrim's Progress*, ch. vi.

Printed in Great Britain by
UNWIN BROTHERS, LIMITED
WOKING AND LONDON

The Christian Revolution Series

Edited by NATHANIEL MICKLEM, M.A., Professor of Old Testament Literature and Theology at the Sely Oak Colleges, Birmingham.

VOLUMES ALREADY ISSUED.

LAY RELIGION. By HENRY T. HODGKIN, M.A., M.B. Cr. 8vo. Second Edition. 4s. net.

THE EARLY CHRISTIAN ATTITUDE TO WAR. A Contribution to the History of Christian Ethics. By C. J. CADOUX, M.A., D.D., Lecturer at Mansfield College, Oxford. With Foreword by the Rev. W. E. ORCHARD, D.D. Cr. 8vo. 10s. 6d. net.

RECONCILIATION AND REALITY. By W. FEARON HALLIDAY, M.A., Winner of the "Large Gold Medal" and First Senior Moderatorship in Mental Science and Moral Science in Trinity College, Dublin. Cr. 8vo. 5s. 6d. net.

THE OPEN LIGHT : An Enquiry into Faith and Reality. By NATHANIEL MICKLEM, M.A. Cr. 8vo. 5s. net.

THE CHRISTIAN IDEAL. By W. E. WILSON, B.D. Cr. 8vo. 5s. 6d. net

THE WAY TO PERSONALITY. By GEORGE B. ROBSON. Third Edition. Cr. 8vo. 5s. 6d. net. Paper covers, 3s. 6d. net.

THE CHRIST OF REVOLUTION. By JOHN R. COATES, B.A. Cr. 8vo. 5s. net. Paper covers, 3s. net.

THE REMNANT. By RUFUS M. JONES, D.Litt. Cr. 8vo. 5s. 6d. net.

MAN AND HIS BUILDINGS. By T. S. ATLEE, M.A., A.R.I.B.A. Illustrated. Cr. 8vo. 6s. net.

THE KINGSHIP OF GOD. By GEORGE B. ROBSON. Cr. 8vo. 6s. 6d. net.

THE MEANING OF PAUL FOR TO-DAY. By PROF. C. H. DODD, M.A. Cr. 8vo. 6s. 6d. net.

CHRIST AND CÆSAR. By N. MICKLEM, M.A., and H. MORGAN, M.A. Cr. 8vo. 6s. 6d. net.

CHRISTIAN JUSTICE. By NORMAN L. ROBINSON, M.A. Cr. 8vo. About 6s. 6d. net (*shortly*).

LONDON: THE SWARTHMORE PRESS, LTD.